CAMPAIGN 285

LEWES AND EVESHAM 1264–65

Simon de Montfort and the Barons' War

RICHARD BROOKS   ILLUSTRATED BY GRAHAM TURNER

Series editor Marcus Cowper

ISBN: 978 1 4728 1150 9
E-book PDF ISBN: 978 1 4728 1151 6
E-pub ISBN: 978 1 4728 1152 3

Editorial by Ilios Publishing Ltd, Oxford, UK (www.iliospublishing.com)
Index by Alan Rutter
Typeset in Myriad Pro and Sabon
Maps by Bounford.com
3D bird's-eye view by The Black Spot
Battlescene illustrations by Graham Turner
Originated by PDQ Media, Bungay, UK
Printed in China through Worldprint Ltd.

15 16 17 18 19   10 9 8 7 6 5 4 3 2 1

ACKNOWLEDGEMENTS

With grateful thanks to the following for their invaluable assistance: Eileen
Brooks, Dave Carson, Marcus Cowper, Nigel Drury, Graham Evans, Graham
Field, Jeff James, Chris Norris, Wendy and Peter Smith, and not least: the
Portsmouth History Centre, Portsmouth Libraries and Archives for access to
their Rolls Series collection.

Prices and Measurements: medieval England used a pre-decimal currency
denominated in pounds, shillings and pence. There were 20 shillings in a
pound, and 12 pence to the shilling. Large amounts were often expressed
in marks worth 13s 4d (£0.67). The text gives significant distances in miles
and kilometres; lesser distances in yards and feet only (90cm and 30cm
respectively).

Sources: the text refers to contemporary authorities by the abbreviated
name of their supposed author or place of writing. See Further Reading for
full titles. Translations from Latin are by the author.

ARTIST'S NOTE

Readers may care to note that the original paintings from which the colour
plates in this book were prepared are available for private sale. The
Publishers retain all reproduction copyright whatsoever. All enquiries
should be addressed to:

Graham Turner, PO Box 568, Aylesbury, Buckinghamshire, HP17 8ZX, UK
www.studio88.co.uk,

The Publishers regret that they can enter into no correspondence upon this
matter.

THE WOODLAND TRUST

Osprey Publishing are supporting the Woodland Trust, the UK's leading
woodland conservation charity, by funding the dedication of trees.

CONTENTS

INTRODUCTION

The battles of Lewes and Evesham, fought in May 1264 and August 1265, were a shocking departure from the political norms of the day. The reign of Henry III (1216–72) was generally peaceful. English wars occurred in Wales or overseas, in England's last Continental possession, Gascony. The last time English knights met in pitched battle on English soil was at Lincoln in 1217, when Henry was a boy of ten.

If Henry's reign was peaceful, it was hardly satisfactory. The conflict known as the Second Barons' War of 1264–65, to distinguish it from the events of 1215–17, arose from longstanding political grievances. A pious and cultured man, Henry III was a feckless and divisive king. He obstinately defended his right to govern, while failing to do so effectively, or to engage the support of his natural counsellors, the baronial elite which controlled the country's landed wealth. Instead, he favoured a succession of foreign adventurers, first the relatives of his wife, Eleanor of Provence, then his Lusignan half-brothers from Poitou, born of Henry's mother's second marriage.

Knightly battle depicted in *La estoire de St Aedward le rei*: contrary to received images of the Middle Ages, such extremes of violence were rare in 13th-century England. (MS Ee.3.59 f.32v by kind permission of the Syndics of Cambridge University Library)

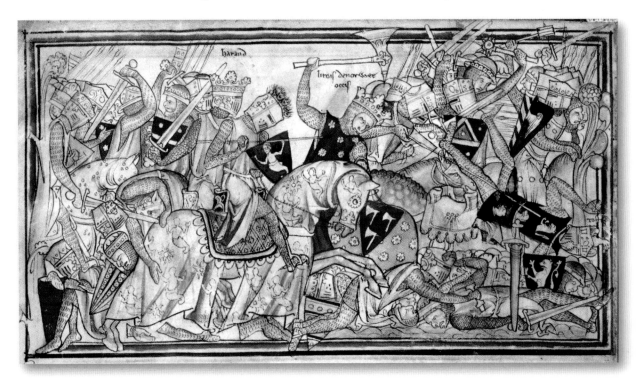

4

The English crown was not rich, and these aliens were resented as intruders, who absorbed rents, lands and ecclesiastical benefices that rightly belonged to native-born Englishmen. The Lusignans' greedy and violent behaviour outraged a burgeoning sense of English identity. All classes shared a distrust of foreigners bordering on xenophobia. New ideas were developing about a community of the realm, no longer limited to the nobility, which distinguished between kings who ruled for the good of their people, and tyrants who did not.

Henry's personal rule might have been more popular had it been more successful. The Poitou campaign of 1242 was a fiasco, amply justifying the English belief that 'Poitevin' meant 'traitor'. Henry's efforts to restrain the unconquered Welsh were hesitant and sometimes disastrous. In 1257 the men of Ystrad Tywi destroyed an English army near Carmarthen leaving several thousand dead, including its commander. A wild scheme to place Henry's second son Edmund on the throne of Sicily was an expensive and embarrassing failure. Royal justices and sheriffs responsible for local administration were considered venal and oppressive, seeking to extract taxes from a countryside racked by famine simply to sustain pointless foreign adventures.

Baronial dissatisfaction with royal misgovernment overflowed in 1258. A parliament of barons and senior churchmen held at Oxford subjected Henry to a counsel nominated by a panel of lay and ecclesiastical magnates. They reduced the king to a cypher, unable to issue writs or charters without their consent. The revolutionary Provisions of Oxford were followed by the Provisions of Westminster addressing judicial abuses. The Lusignans were expelled, and offices such as the custodianship of royal castles were restricted to Englishmen.

Henry's subjection to baronial oversight was unsustainable. The magnates split between reformers and conservatives, and in 1261 Henry reasserted his freedom with support from the Pope and 500 knights paid by Henry's brother-in-law, Louis IX of France. The only magnate left to defend the Provisions was Simon de Montfort, Earl of Leicester. Rather than break his oath he left England, but returned two years later after further dissension. Simon reimposed the Provisions, but his faction was too weak to dominate an unwilling king.

Henry III's main interests were artistic. His greatest achievement was rebuilding Westminster Abbey, where he is commemorated by this early 14th-century painting in the Sedilia. (Copyright Dean and Chapter Westminster)

Baronial in origin, the movement might now be styled Montfortian, or even rebel.

Law and order collapsed, as both sides attacked each others' manors and estates. The Londoners seized the organs of national government, imprisoning judges and Treasury officials. The king's eldest son, the Lord Edward, besieged Montfortian castles in South Wales and pillaged the Marches, 'much harm was done on both sides' (Walsingham). Cornered at Gloucester, Edward escaped by swearing false oaths. So disturbed was the kingdom, said the Waverley Annals, with fresh calamities every day, that anyone might see it could not be settled without a battle.

These were rare events; knightly battles were almost as scarce as fleet actions between dreadnought battleships. Outcomes were unpredictable, and the risks extreme, especially for commanders. William Marshal, the victor of Lincoln, fought only four pitched battles in a military career lasting over five decades. His opposite number at Lincoln was stabbed through his helmet's eye-slits. Lewes and Evesham were the only significant battles fought by English armies in the mid-13th century, our only evidence for how the English fought before the longbow became the national weapon.

The preceding strategic manoeuvres have excited much admiration as precocious examples of the interplay of internal and external lines, royal commanders seeking to exploit a central position between divided baronial forces, to crush them separately. They succeeded for a while, in 1264, capturing Northampton and several Midland castles before Simon could march to their relief. When the royalists moved south, however, they allowed him to concentrate his forces, and defeat them at Lewes. Simon's narrow margin of success denied him an outright political victory. Key supporters changed sides, provoking a renewed struggle in the following spring. This time the royal commanders succeeded. Simon was caught at Evesham with part of his army, defeated and killed.

Unlike most medieval conflicts, the Second Barons' War was decided not by ravaging and attrition, but by manoeuvre and battle. The location of its battles has inspired extensive debate, on which fresh evidence has recently cast fresh light. Their dramatically different outcome helped shape English constitutional and political developments for centuries.

Simon de Montfort's appearance is unknown, like that of most medieval people. The 20th-century monument in Lewes Priory shows him bearded and resolute, wearing anachronistic plate armour. (Author's photograph: original sculpture Enzo Piazotta)

CHRONOLOGY

1264

3 April	Henry III raises the Royal Standard at Oxford.
5 April	Attacks and captures Northampton.
11 April	Takes Leicester.
12 April	Occupies Nottingham.
17 April	Simon attacks Rochester.
20 April	Henry III marches south to relieve Rochester.
26 April	Simon withdraws to London.
2 May	Henry III marches into the Weald.
6 May	Simon leaves London seeking battle.
9 May	Henry III at Winchelsea: hears Simon has left London.
10–11 May	Henry III marches to Lewes.
14 May	BATTLE OF LEWES.

1265

January	Simon calls first parliament to include knights of shires and burgesses.
April	Henry III's exiled supporters land at Pembroke.
8 May	Simon moves to Hereford.
28 May	Edward escapes from Hereford and joins Mortimer at Wigmore.
29 May	Agrees Treaty of Ludlow with Clare and Mortimer.
14 June	Royalists take Gloucester trapping Simon west of River Severn.
19 June	Simon agrees treaty of Pipton with Llewelyn of Wales.
24 June	Simon marches into South Wales.
28 June	Simon summons Younger Simon.
4–8 July	Edward and Clare cut Simon off at Newport.
16–18 July	Simon regains Hereford; Younger Simon sacks Winchester.
31 July	Younger Simon arrives at Kenilworth.
1 August	Edward marches to Kenilworth overnight.
2 August	Edward attacks Younger Simon's army at dawn and returns to Worcester.
	Simon leaves Hereford and crosses Severn at Kempsey.
3 August	Simon marches for Evesham overnight; Edward leaves Worcester.
4 August	BATTLE OF EVESHAM.
28 October	Simon's widow surrenders Dover Castle and sails for France.
23 November	Younger Simon surrenders Axholme.

1266

10 February	Younger Simon flees abroad.
15 May	Battle of Chesterfield.
24–25 June	Henry III besieges Kenilworth Castle.
31 October	Dictum of Kenilworth.
20 December	Kenilworth Castle surrenders.

OPPOSING COMMANDERS

Medieval command structures were loose and consensual, held together by social ties of kinship, affinity and fealty. Plans ascribed to Henry III or Simon de Montfort for narrative convenience may well represent a group position. English commanders of the 1260s were leaders more than generals, commanding from the front. Often seen as unpractised, they were neither irrational nor unskilled, their military skills honed from childhood by chivalric activities such as hunting and jousting. Ceaselessly perambulating their own or their lord's estates, they developed a natural eye for country that supplied the want of maps. Leaders at Lewes and Evesham clearly understood the tactical value of ground, the use of reserves and surprise.

ROYALIST COMMANDERS

Edmund Ironside and Cnut portrayed by Matthew Paris, watched by their armies: chivalric warfare was less individualistic than this 13-century painting might suggest. (MS 26 80v by kind permission of the Master and Fellows of Corpus Christi College Cambridge)

As king, **Henry III** was the natural head of the royalists, *regales* or *reaulx*, as contemporaries styled them. He was, however, as Walter of Guisborough put it, '*vir simplex, pacificus non bellicosus*', 'a naïve man, peaceful not warlike'. Peter of Langtoft remembered him as 'a good man always … kind to the poor'. Henry preferred fine arts to fighting, perhaps reacting against the alarms of his childhood during the First Barons' War. Henry gave a convincing

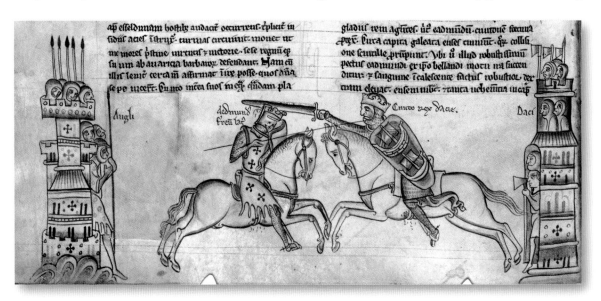

display of military incapacity at Taillebourg during the Poitou expedition, allowing his French opponents to stage an opposed river crossing, an astonishing feat for a medieval army. An infuriated Simon de Montfort suggested afterwards that Henry should be locked up like the unfortunate Carolingian monarch, Charles the Simple.

Henry III has suffered a bad press. Most English chroniclers of his day took an anti-government line, inspired by King John's monastic depredations, confirmed by Henry's generosity to foreign churchmen. Even the royalist Thomas Wykes denied Henry credit for the dynamic strategy pursued in his name during the spring of 1264, saying he trusted, 'in the resolute courage of his eldest son'. Wounded at Lewes, Henry was forced to capitulate. Next year he was still in enemy hands, unable to influence events. Rescued at Evesham, he failed to restrain his followers' greedy exploitation of victory, ensuring continued disorder.

Henry III in full armour, as shown on the royal seal. His record as a military leader was poor, and would not be enhanced by the Barons' War. (Original drawing courtesy of Eileen Brooks

The mainspring of the royalist cause is generally agreed to have been Henry's eldest son, the **Lord Edward** (1239–1307). As Edward I he would extinguish Welsh independence, and achieve a fearsome reputation as Hammer of the Scots. Wykes described him as an 'invincible warrior giant'. Edward possessed immense energy, seeking to renew the battle of Lewes, driving his men through two night marches in the three days before Evesham. Modern views of Edward may be coloured by his subsequent career. Wykes' rival historiographer at Osney Priory neglected Edward's part in the events before Evesham, subordinating him to the turncoat Gilbert of Clare, Earl of Gloucester. The *Cambridge Medieval History* unkindly suggests Edward's successes depended on his enemies' neglect of basic military precautions. More than one commentator has condemned Edward's impetuous pursuit at Lewes, which may have lost the battle.

Unlike his father, Edward was devious and ruthless. The Dunstable annalist claims he twice broke sworn agreements with junior de Montforts: Henry at Gloucester in 1264 and Simon the Younger at Axholme the following year. Under open arrest at Hereford in April 1265, Edward fooled his minders into tiring their own horses, before escaping on a fresh mount. His deception measures before Evesham still confuse historians. In the ensuing battle, Simon was brutally eliminated, preventing a repetition of the indecisive outcome of Lewes. Edward avoided blame for the massacre, shedding well-recorded tears over the corpse of Henry de Montfort with whom he grew up. His annihilation of the baronial leadership foreshadows his pitiless harrying of Welsh princes and Scottish resistance leaders.

A less well-known contributor to royal counsels was Henry III's brother, **Richard Earl of Cornwall** (1209–72). Sometimes styled 'King of Rome' following his election as heir to the German Emperor, Richard was more diplomat than soldier. Leading an English Crusade to the Holy Land in 1240, he secured the release of captive French knights, exploiting their gratitude to extricate Henry from the Taillebourg debacle. At Lewes, Richard led the royalist centre, was trapped in a windmill, and captured. Kept hostage in 1265, the rebels released him after Evesham as a mediator.

Roger Mortimer (1231–82), lord of Wigmore Castle in the Welsh marches, was implacably opposed to the Earl of Leicester, who sought to accommodate the Welsh prince Llewelyn ap Gruffudd, the Marchers' deadly enemy. Described as 'a knight proven in military matters', Mortimer was released after Lewes to defend the Marches, but made no effort to work with de Montfort's government. Instrumental in Edward's escape in April 1265, he saw action in all the major engagements of the war. As Simon's killer, he became one of Edward I's closest post-war associates.

BARONIAL COMMANDERS

The Lord Edward in later life as depicted outside Lincoln Cathedral with Queen Eleanor. His dynamic leadership during the Barons' War set the tone for his reign as Edward I. (Author's photograph)

The predominant figure on either side was **Simon de Montfort**, Earl of Leicester, whose unwavering determination drove the conflict to its tragic denouement. Ironically, Simon was another foreign adventurer, owing his fortune to royal favour. Born in France, he was the penniless younger son of another Simon de Montfort: leader of the Albigensian Crusade against the Cathars, victor of the battle of Muret, decapitated by a mangonel shot outside Toulouse. His son inherited several paternal attributes: military competence, austere faith, unflinching obstinacy, and a claim to the Earldom of Leicester, which he made good in the 1230s. He also gained the hand of Henry III's sister Eleanor. The Second Baron's War was a family affair.

As late as 1244, Simon mediated between king and parliament. Later that decade, the Lusignans ousted him from royal favour, while an ill-fated Seneschalship of Gascony divided the brothers-in-law. Relations became so hostile that Henry wished Simon a similar death to his father, another 'inciter and lover of war'. Simon became the Provisions' leading sponsor, and head of the reform movement as other magnates fell away.

Even Simon's critics admired his military ability. Wykes said he marched on Lewes, 'with no less art than strength'. A narrative of the two battles attributed to William Rishanger, a monk at St Albans, praised Simon's siege of Rochester as something unknown in England. At Lewes, it was the Earl who arrayed the baronial host, the English being ignorant of military discipline. The pro-Montfortian Waverley Annals styled him *miles emeritus*, a veteran knight. The moderate Westminster Chronicle described him as, 'most noble and well tried in military matters'. Writing 50 years later, Rishanger says Simon 'spent his time in warlike assemblies from the flowering of his youth, most expertly gaining eternally celebrated fame in many regions'. He accompanied Richard of Cornwall to the Holy Land, where he was said to have been offered guardianship of the rump Kingdom of Jerusalem, perhaps the most challenging command in Christendom. Subsequently, Simon conducted military operations in Wales and Gascony. At Lewes he led from behind, commanding a reserve, as his father had done at Muret.

Simon brought the reform movement moral strength, as well as generalship. Rishanger's Chronicle characterized him as 'constant in word, severe in aspect'. Others describe him as *vir ille magnificus* and 'Man of God'. Simon's unflustered reaction to his son's capture in the war's opening engagement at Northampton demonstrates his steadfastness, 'not despairing, knowing it to be the law of war that now these now those, through altered circumstances, should be superior' (ibid.). Simon's political vision may have stemmed from his friend Robert Grosseteste (d. 1253), Bishop of Lincoln and England's foremost thinker. Author of a treatise on tyranny that Simon may have read, Grosseteste had no illusions about his friend's unbending character, prophesying a death like his father's, for justice and truth. The struggle for the Provisions became a Crusade, pursued to the bitter end.

The baronial faction's greatest weakness was its lack of magnates, which drove Simon to rely on his sons before they were equal to the task. The hostile Wykes commented that one was 'recently girdled with the belt of knighthood, no half-hearted emulator of his ancestor's insolence'. Henry, the eldest, rarely held independent command. He led the baronial right at Lewes, and died with his father at Evesham. His younger brother Simon (d. 1271), 'who first raised a standard against the king', played a more independent role. Captured at Northampton in April 1264, he is accused of throwing away the Evesham campaign. Responding too slowly to his father's summons, he suffered avoidable losses outside Kenilworth Castle, and missed the battle.

The chief magnate to fight alongside de Montfort was **Gilbert de Clare, Earl of Gloucester** (1243–95). He did so for personal reasons; Henry III had denied him his inheritance, because he was not yet 21. Alienated by Simon's aggrandizement after Lewes, de Clare changed sides to play a crucial part in the royalist revival. He isolated the older Simon beyond the River Severn, took a leading part in Edward's spoiling attack on Kenilworth, and led the royalist left wing at Evesham. Rishanger suggests de Clare learned his tactics from Simon at Lewes, but he may have owed his eminence more to social position than ability. Edward I dismissed him as Warden of South and West Wales in 1277, following an ambush in which Edward's Poitevin cousin William de Valence was killed. A weathercock who changed sides five times in as many years, de Clare finally restored peace by occupying London, to soften the king's stance towards surviving rebels.

OPPOSING FORCES

Thirteenth-century armies were transient affairs. They left few administrative traces, especially during civil wars when government machinery broke down. Of the three elements that constitute an order of battle – numbers, organization and equipment – only the latter can be described with any certainty for Lewes and Evesham. Not until the reign of Henry III's successor does sufficient record evidence, such as documents listing the value of combatants' horses, survive to control the claims of chroniclers. These are at best hearsay, at worst fantasy. Organization and equipment are less problematic. In many ways, the two sides were similar. The conflict was a political dispute between aristocratic factions, not a social revolution mobilizing new kinds of forces. Many of the comments about the royal forces apply equally to their opponents.

ROYALIST FORCES

The army that fought for Henry III at Lewes was assembled by royal writ in the traditional way. The king sent out messengers to all parts of the kingdom with letters summoning all those 'holding to him' to come to Oxford with horse and arms in the middle of Quadragesima. Oxford was conveniently central. Most of the English population inhabited the Midlands, and everyone would know the date of the first Sunday in Lent. Northern reinforcements joined at Nottingham, where the king celebrated Easter. How many responded to Henry's call we do not know. When he summoned a similar host to besiege Kenilworth Castle in 1266 many of those owing military service excused themselves, saying they had already gone *in expeditionem* three or four times in the previous 12 months, contrary to statute.

The Evesham campaign required an alternative approach, the king being in baronial custody. Then the royalist leaders used 'copious bribes

Knightly equipment is better documented than medieval administration, thanks to monuments such as William de Valence's effigy at Dorchester Abbey. One of Henry III's Poitevin relations, William was killed by the Welsh in 1282. (Photograph courtesy of Graham Field, The Medieval Combat Society (www.themcs.org))

and promises' to mobilize their supporters, and anyone else with a grudge against de Montfort's regime, 'so all the Marchers, and the Earl of Gloucester, and the fugitives, and friends of the prisoners came in great strength, and in short formed a powerful army' (Rishanger). Thomas Wykes confirms that the Lord Edward's army consisted of disaffected Marchers and Poitevins recently landed at Pembroke, 'with a following of bold warriors', and 'an innumerable multitude of knights from the adjoining parts of the kingdom', in other words the West Midlands. With Gloucester's followers, they formed 'such a force of horse and foot beyond estimation of its strength that it inspired astonishment in his allies and fear in his enemies'. The Marchers mattered; whatever applied elsewhere in England they spent their lives fighting the Welsh, becoming a battle-hardened elite. The Furness Chronicle describes them as 'distinguished men-at-arms, well tried in arms'.

The tactical organisation of these forces can be assumed to follow the usual medieval pattern. Groups of relatives and friends formed *conrois* or 'banners' of ten to twenty men each. These then joined up with several others to make an *eschiele* or 'battle'. Perhaps 100 strong, they were convenient units to deploy in line abreast or one behind another, as William Marshal had formed his divisions at Lincoln. Bound together by kinship and amity they enjoyed a cohesion that later centuries had to instil on the parade ground. Latinate monks wrote of *cohorts* and *turmae*, but this is as misleading as their references to multitudes.

Such evidence as we have suggests knightly armies were tiny. The medieval population was small and poor; knightly equipment and training expensive. A knight's outfit might cost the annual output of a village. Henry III's grandfather Henry II conducted a survey in 1166 which identified just 6,278 English knight's fees, the territorial units owing a mounted warrior's service. A century later, the figure had dwindled to 1,000 or 2,000. Fewer still would turn out for a civil war. The Committee of 25 appointed to oversee King John's adherence to Magna Carta promised to provide 1,187 knights between them, ranging from seven to 200 each. At Lincoln the Marshal disposed of 406 knights, 317 crossbows, and a few hundred sergeants, non-noble heavy cavalry. Edward I mobilized several thousand mounted men for his Welsh and Scottish campaigns, but these were national efforts. England in the 1260s was divided and unenthusiastic. Many of the arms-bearing class must have kept their heads down, as they did in King John's time. Lack of numbers mattered in more ways than one. Small armies were mobile; easy to move and supply, they occupied little space on the battlefield; vulnerable to surprise and lacking reserves of combat power, they might be quickly defeated.

Military equipment reflected the wealth and social class of those wearing it. Statutes known as the Assize of Arms laid down

The forces of evil line up behind the many-headed beast from the Book of Revelations. Note the closely serried ranks, the bannerets, and the varied headgear. (MS R.16.2 f23r by kind permission of the Master and Fellows of Trinity College Cambridge)

the gear appropriate to different economic groups, although how far statutory requirements were met is uncertain. The 1242 Assize required those at the top, holders of land worth £15 a year, to possess a long mail coat or *lorica*, iron cap, sword, dagger and horse, as should those with goods worth £40. Lances and shields were not specified, being consumable items. Well-equipped knights needed more than one horse, riding cheaper palfreys to battle to keep their expensive chargers or *destriers* in good condition. Until it was needed, armour was carried on pack horses or rounceys ridden by page boys, allowing rapid movement.

Legislation set a minimum standard, neglecting to specify the padded *pourpoint* or gambeson worn beneath the *lorica* to prevent chafing and absorb blows. Neither did it mention the small pieces of plate armour that protected vulnerable points such as knees and elbows, or the horse armour sometimes dissimulated beneath armorial trappings. Horses had worn mail protection since at least 1198 when 140 of the 200 French knights Richard I captured at Gisors had 'covered horses'. A similar proportion was current in Italy during the 1250s. Knights concerned more with protection than visibility replaced the iron cap with a cylindrical great helm or *galea*, as seen on Henry III's royal seal. Many combatants must have counted as sergeants, wearing the simpler protection demanded of the less wealthy, the *hebergetum* or shorter mail shirt of the £10 landholder, even the *pourpoint* of the £5 man, although the Assize does not refer to their being horsed.

One of medieval England's greatest crimes, the murder of Thomas Becket, as depicted in the 1250s. Note the mail hauberks split for riding, the middle knight's coif looped up under the chin. (Author's collection)

The proportion of footmen to horse is uncertain. In 1205 Dunstable Priory had contributed one *lorica*, nine *loricella* (shorter mail shirts), and 11 *pourpoints* to the national defences. This implies a one-to-ten ratio of mounted men to foot, if one *pourpoint* was worn as padding. Chronicle references to hundreds of knights and thousands of infantry at Lewes and Evesham suggest a similar multiple. The defeated army at Lincoln in 1217, however, fielded 600 mounted men to just over 1,000 infantry, a proportion nearer the 'four men … with horse and arms, and six footmen' that Dunstable Priory sent for coastal defence in 1264. Pay records for Edward I's Falkirk campaign in 1298 show 2,500 mounted troops against 14,800 English and Irish foot, a ratio of one to six. Such large numbers were exceptional, however. Edwardian armies in Wales rarely exceeded 3,000–4,000 infantry. Infantry weapons specified by the Assize of Arms included spears for the £5 men in *pourpoints*; bows and arrows for the unarmoured 40 shilling men; lesser arms such as *falces* and *gisarmes* for the rest – falchions and billhooks. Henry III's Scottish vassals are said to have brought large numbers of foot south with them in 1264. If equipped like the Scottish infantry who fought his grandson, they wore quilted linen armour, 'which a sword would not readily penetrate', with spears in their hands and axes at their sides (*Vita Edwardi II*).

The 1242 Assize was the first to mention what would soon become the English national weapon. There are no references to its battlefield use in 1264–65, although Rishanger mentions bows and crossbows at the siege of Rochester. Henry III clearly employed mercenary crossbowmen. Royal records show them agreeing ransom terms with a man-at-arms captured at Northampton. Legal cases arising from accidental killings prove that bows and arrows were common. King John raised many archers in the 1213 invasion scare, though he never used them in the field. Matthew Paris included numerous archers and slingers in his battle scenes during the years just before the Baron's War. University students with slings, bows and crossbows opposed Henry III's entering of Oxford in 1264. Later that year, Henry executed 300 Kentish archers after one shot his cook. Large numbers of archers were mobilized in the summer after Lewes, four or eight per village. Three hundred of them garrisoned Winchelsea; more appear at Dover.

Most combatants at Lewes and Evesham were infantry. Protection might be a short mail shirt or a padded gambeson, right and left, worn interchangeably with round iron caps or kettle hats. (Original watercolour courtesy of Eileen Brooks)

It is puzzling, therefore, that no archers feature at Lewes or Evesham. Perhaps they were dispersed among the other foot, unable to generate the concentrated arrow storms of later battles, the archers' line of sight obscured by the knights in front. Perhaps English armies were too well protected with their mail and gambesons, unlike the naked Manxmen slaughtered by Anglo-Scots slingers, archers and crossbowmen near Russin Abbey in 1274. There is, of course, no archaeological or linguistic basis for the notion that the English peasantry adopted an improved long bow sometime after Evesham, whether spontaneously or by copying the Welsh. The weapon is known throughout as *arcus*, regardless of its supposed length, which remains constant from the Dark Ages.

BARONIAL FORCES

Henry III's opponents mustered, organized and equipped their core forces in much the same way as the royalists. Regarding himself as the legitimate government, Simon used royal writs to summon a host to Worcester when fresh hostilities threatened in May 1265. The decisive difference between the sides was the number of men raised, although verifiable figures are lacking. Chroniclers agree the barons were outnumbered: by four to one at Lewes according to the Dunstable annalist; more so at Evesham.

De Montfort's support evaporated as the reform movement splintered. Possessing numerical parity with Henry III's supporters in 1258, the barons were increasingly divided. Simon was left fatally dependent on his family and Midland associates, such as the unrelated Peter de Montfort. As with the baronial opposition to King John, many dissidents were younger men with nothing to lose, for example the younger Humphrey de Bohun, the Earl of Hereford's son, who was wounded at both battles. Wykes derisively styled them 'boys'. Such men lacked the military resources of the great feudatories, underlining the decisive nature of Gloucester's defection. In 1251, Simon was owed the service of just 60 knights' fees from his earldom. At the height of his power, he celebrated Christmas 1264 with 160 paid knights, *milites stipendarios* (Rishanger).

To make up his numbers, Simon appealed to the lesser gentry, propelled into opposition by local grievances, xenophobia and the indebtedness that inspired their attacks on the Jews. Perhaps half the gentry of Northamptonshire, in de Montfort's heartland, supported him compared with a sixth who held to the king. Almost 80 of Simon's supporters are known by name, compared with less than 30 royalists, but that is no sure guide to the number of hooves on the ground. The closest any contemporary comes to a Montfortian order of battle is the statement by two Yorkshire sources (the Melsa and Lanercost Chronicles) that baronial losses at Evesham amounted to 180 knights, 200 other men-at-arms, 5,000 Welsh, and 2,000 other foot. If they are confusing start strength with casualties, a simple error, Simon's numbers, excluding the Welsh, had been roughly halved since Lewes.

De Montfort supplemented his conventional forces in other ways. In happier times the king had entrusted him with castles at Leicester, Odiham in Hampshire and Kenilworth near Warwick. Throughout the struggle he controlled Dover, long considered 'the gateway to England'. Further castles were entrusted to supporters during his dictatorship, for example Portchester, which controlled Portsmouth Harbour, went to his son. Along with London, these fortified places provided refuges and strategic pivots of manoeuvre. Resenting Henry's arbitrary taxes and a planned fair at Westminster, London was staunchly anti-royalist. After Lewes the Lord Mayor even had the impudence to make his loyalty conditional on the king's continued good lordship.

Besides shelter, London provided troops, a tradition dating from the siege of Winchester in 1141, when 1,000 Londoners marched down to Hampshire, 'magnificently equipped with helmets and coats of mail'. Rich merchants presumably qualified for the well-armoured top end of the Assize of Arms. When Henry III approached the city in 1264, the citizens came out,

Castles substituted for the Montfortians' lack of numbers, allowing them to dominate the Midlands. Kenilworth Castle, seen here, was a royal castle, built by King John, entrusted to Simon in happier days. (Author's photograph)

'not however to receive him with palms [it being Easter], but to repel him with spears' (Guisborough). The Londoners' showing was less impressive at Lewes, where the Waverley Annals commented on their lack of military experience, 'for seeing the battle they took themselves off in flight'. Wykes dismissed them as 'an immense mass ignorant of combat', the city providing 'an inexhaustible supply of fools ready for anything'. They made a better show at Rochester, the Canterbury chronicler styling them 'proven soldiers, mostly nobly defending their city'. Their absence at Evesham may have been decisive.

Less conventional allies came from Kent where the mariners of the Cinque Ports proved 'undaunted rebels'. Controlling the maritime resources of the south-east coast, this coterie of south coast towns could interdict Henry III's communications with his French and Papal backers. When the king marched down to compel their obedience, the men of Winchelsea took ship with their families and possessions, and sailed away. Equally slippery were the archers of the Kentish Weald, the ancient forest which lay west of the prosperous Watling Street corridor, filling the great valley between the South Downs and the Surrey Hills. As in 1217, its undeveloped woodland, sparse population and poor roads made the Weald a hostile environment for conventional forces. Unlike their ancestors who overran French detachments outside Lewes and Dover, the Weald men of 1264 restricted themselves to guerrilla warfare, harassing passing royalists as if resenting the presence of any armed intruder.

De Montfort's other irregular allies were the Welsh he obtained from Llewelyn ap Gruffudd by the Treaty of Pipton. These may have been more trouble than they were worth. Lightly armed spearmen from North Wales had a mixed record outside their cavalry-proof hills and forests. Cut to pieces at the First Battle of Lincoln in 1141, they did better in Henry II's reign attacking French supply wagons during the siege of Rouen, only to be annihilated after his defeat at Le Mans in 1189. Their presence in Simon's ranks confirmed the Marchers' diehard opposition, before swelling the casualty list at Evesham.

One unconventional resource on both sides were the spies or scouts who provided the intelligence required for the strategic cut and thrust of the Evesham campaign. It was *per exploratores* that de Montfort avoided an ambush laid by his shifty ally the Earl of Gloucester outside Hereford in May 1265. The royalist strike against the younger Simon at Kenilworth required 'skilful scouts', who not only betrayed his exposed position outside the castle, but found his men still abed: tactical as well as strategic reconnaissance. So accepted was the presence of spies, the royalists had employed lavish deception measures to conceal their destination. The subsequent interception of the older Simon at Evesham was similarly intelligence led. Neither side were the myopic blunderers of popular legend.

Both sides in the Barons' War used foreign auxiliaries: Henry III's northern supporters brought numerous Scots infantry to Lewes, on left; Simon deployed Welsh infantry at Evesham, centre and right. (Original watercolour courtesy of Eileen Brooks)

OPPOSING PLANS

Our understanding of the strategies that led to Lewes and Evesham derives from the protagonists' behaviour rather than recorded statements of intent. Beyond a few hints from chroniclers not much better informed than us, we have no direct evidence for either side's intentions. No trace survives of the heated debates we know preceded other battles such as Bouvines in 1214. This does not mean they did not happen in the 1260s. The royal leaders met in Lewes Priory on the morning of the battle, witnessed a document and presumably discussed their options. The knighting ceremonies that preceded both major actions provided further opportunities for consultation.

The planning process is obscured by a mixture of contemporary bias and modern contempt for medieval strategists. Wykes attributed de Montfort's attack on Rochester in April 1264 to anger at his son's capture at Northampton, rather than more rational motives. The *Cambridge Medieval History* claims that 'in strategy feudal armies displayed even less advance than in tactics'. Lack of documentary evidence makes it difficult

Medieval decision-making was collegial, plans thrashed out in public spaces such as the Great Hall at Winchester, the only remaining part of the castle where Henry III was born. (Postcard from Author's collection)

to say how far strategic choices were made in advance, or in reaction to changing circumstance. Nevertheless, commentators on both Lewes and Evesham have detected the interplay between internal and external lines of operation as first one side then the other tried to make the enemy dance to their tune. In both campaigns the royalists were concentrated and sought to defeat the enemy's divided forces separately: in 1264 they failed; in 1265 they succeeded.

Underpinning both sides' manoeuvres were a number of fixed points. Towns, manors and castles formed a network of familiar locations that provided security, food, and communications links. Henry III chose Lewes for its castle, which belonged to John de Warenne, Earl of Surrey and Sussex, who served in the royal host. Simon mustered nearby at his own woodland manor of Fletching. When he crossed the river Severn the following year, he did so at a manor belonging to his ally the Bishop of Worcester. The younger Simon should have moved his troops inside Kenilworth Castle. Evesham's lack of defences made disaster inevitable.

ROYALIST PLANS

The *Cambridge Medieval History* dismissed Henry III's opening strategy as 'an aimless attempt at the reduction of castles, in which he deliberately threw away his chance of making for a definite objective, and left the field clear for his adversary'. This seems unfair. The choice of Oxford for the royalist rendezvous in April 1264 divided his opponents and facilitated the junction of the king's entourage from Windsor with Edward's flying column fresh from plundering Gloucester. Parties from Oxford went to secure Reigate and Rochester, whose castles guarded the routes south and south-east of London. Then the main body marched north to liquidate baronial support in the Midlands, and meet royalist reinforcements from the North. Given Henry's lamentable performance in Poitou, this purposeful scheme is usually attributed to the canny Richard of Cornwall or the dynamic Lord Edward. All the chroniclers say is that the king took counsel of his men, in the customary manner.

Riding northwards interposed the royal host between Simon's main army in London, and his supporters in the Midlands and East Anglia. The threat to destroy his allies piecemeal may have been intended to tempt Simon out to give battle at a numerical disadvantage. If that were so, the calculation nearly paid off. Simon had marched as far as St Albans when he heard that Northampton had fallen. When the royalists turned south to relieve Rochester, they ensured strategic ambiguity was maintained. Crossing the Thames at Kingston they could threaten London or Rochester with equal ease, while snapping up the Earl of Gloucester's local castles. The royalists' subsequent advance into Kent, however, cost them their central position, allowing Simon to concentrate against them at Lewes.

The royalist leaders pursued a similar strategy the following year. Quickly seizing a central position in the Severn Valley, they isolated Simon at Hereford, west of the river, far from his supporters in eastern England. Breaking down the bridges, they intercepted Montfortian messengers, and patrolled the Bristol Channel with galleys. At the same time, they pursued a logistical strategy to starve Simon out, denying him victuals and reinforcements.

Royalist strategy in 1265 centred on the Severn, England's greatest river. Royalist control of crossings at Worcester (shown here) and elsewhere divided Montfortian forces, and denied the older Simon food and reinforcements. (Postcard from Author's collection)

To defeat an enemy in detail demands mobility. The speed of royalist movements before Lewes and Evesham bears comparison with other 13th-century campaigns, but has been exaggerated. Wykes describes their host as 'flying across the counties, pressing on through the night almost without sleep'. Rishanger claimed they made such speed, 'the choicest horses fell dead, exhausted by the effort'. Henry III's march south in April 1264 was nothing exceptional: 80 miles (120km) from Grantham to Aylesbury in five days was much the same daily rate as his unhurried two-day march from Windsor to Oxford in March. The final stages around London were more demanding, 80 miles in two days, a speed only possible with mounted troops.

Edward's overnight march from Worcester to Kenilworth covered similar distances: 35 miles (56km) in the eight hours from dusk to dawn. These march rates compare with those achieved in the First Barons' War where on occasion both sides marched 26 to 28 miles (42–45km) per day over several days. Fast-moving armies could arrive before news of their coming, catching the enemy unawares. Approach marches to Evesham were shorter, 12½ miles (20km) as the crow flies. The royalists owed their final victory to timely and well-directed marches, not just long ones.

BARONIAL PLANS

The Barons' strategic problem was the converse of the royalists': outnumbered and divided, they had to wait and see what the enemy did next. The same hesitancy affected their opening moves in both campaigns, reflecting political as well as military weakness. After a faltering start in 1264, Simon launched a lightning riposte to crush the royalists at Lewes. The following year his difficulties proved insuperable.

The river Usk and Newport Castle (right of bridge): Simon marched into South Wales to outflank the royalist blockade, but enemy land forces cut him off at Newport while their galleys sank his ships. (Postcard from Author's collection)

Rebel strategy suffered a basic contradiction between dispersal to protect their territorial base, and the need to concentrate against a stronger enemy. Unable or unwilling to risk battle in April 1264, Simon distributed his forces to protect his power-base in the Midlands and the capital, the loss of which would have been fatal. Leaving his sons Simon and Henry to defend Northampton and Kenilworth, he went to London, which provided a secure base for his manoeuvres throughout the campaign. Wykes believed the Northampton rebels were awaiting the opportune moment when 'having drawn together their men from various parts, they might transfer themselves to their chief, the Earl of Leicester, who had occupied all London by a similar piece of effrontery'.

After Henry III's march to Nottingham had disappointed baronial expectations of a royalist drive on London, Simon regained the initiative by attacking Rochester. Like William Marshal before Lincoln, Henry III could not afford the political cost of losing a major stronghold without a fight. Unlike the Marshal's opponents, Simon was too wary to be caught *in flagrante*, and retreated to London. When the royalists marched into Sussex, Simon followed with all his remaining forces, including those from Kenilworth, and deliberately sought battle. This was unusual. Battles were risky, and barons rarely challenged kings in the open field. Civil wars were an exception, however, landowners being anxious to stop their estates being ravaged. Simon was also exceptional: a royal brother-in-law, inflamed with moral righteousness, convinced that God was on his side. Politically he had little choice but to fight. Henry III had repeatedly demonstrated his refusal to accept any diminution of royal authority, regardless of his promises to the contrary.

Simon's hesitancy the following year was exacerbated by the unfavourable balance of forces that followed de Clare's defection. Nevertheless, Montfortian strategy in 1265 was not dissimilar to that of the previous year. Wykes comments more than once on Simon's anxiety to regain London. A rare letter suggests he hoped to mount a pincer movement against Edward's Marcher army at Gloucester in June. When this failed to materialize, Simon marched to Newport in South Wales to outflank the royalists, and regain touch with Simon the Younger by sea, an imaginative concept for its own or any day. When that attempt also failed, the de Montforts reverted to their original scheme whereby the younger Simon would divert Edward, and let the older Simon cross the Severn.

The plan was partly successful: the Severn was crossed, but the diversionary force suffered crippling losses outside Kenilworth. The older Simon stuck to his plan, marching east to join his son at Evesham. Once united there, sat astride the main Worcester–London road that runs south of the river, he might have regained the initiative as he had at Lewes. Otherwise, it is hard to understand his entering the Evesham pocket, encircled as it is by a major river but open on the north towards his son's expected approach. Poor reconnaissance and the notorious difficulties of coordinating widely separated columns caused the younger Simon to miss the rendezvous, with fatal results for his father.

Underlying the deliberate manoeuvres of leaders struggling for strategic advantage was a wave of unscripted violence directed against all and sundry. This was not just a pointless distraction from the war's wider purposes. It was a constant feature of chivalric warfare, the hope of plunder being a necessary inducement for the unpaid rank and file. It might also condition the political responses of the highest in the land. The moderate Richard of Cornwall was angered 'beyond measure' by the Londoners' destruction of his manor at Isleworth, an outrage that fuelled his vehement rejection of Simon's last peace overtures before Lewes.

Both sides used devastation to punish their opponents. The Lord Edward spread misery and destruction around the disloyal Earl Ferrars' Derbyshire manors. De Montfort's government ravaged the Archbishop of Canterbury's

Pillage and devastation were essential features of all medieval wars, intended to bring home the economic cost of resistance to the enemy: 13th-century knights driving off cattle and pack animals. (Author's collection)

estates after his unauthorized departure overseas. Supply arrangements were essentially pillage: Simon the Younger sacked Winchester when the city refused his weary troops entry, 'although some of his men were falling down under his own eyes'. Few citizens were killed, but their movable goods were thoroughly plundered. Extortion spilled over into atrocity. The Furness Chronicle reported one specimen incident. A party of royalists ravaged the manor of a knight from the baronial party and drove off his beasts. Returning with a few men, the owner caught seven looters in one of his houses, and burned it to the ground with them still inside. As Rishanger complained after Lewes, 'The whole year, for five months and two weeks, trembled with the hardships of war; and while everyone took care to defend his castle, every neighbourhood was depopulated, devastating the fields, carrying off the cattle, in defence of the castles, nor were churches and cemeteries spared. Moreover, the houses of the very poorest peasants, were turned over and plundered, even to the bed straw' (Chronicle).

THE LEWES CAMPAIGN

THE CAPTURE OF NORTHAMPTON

Open warfare began in the first week of April 1264, after the customary rituals. Absolved by the Pope from his oath to observe the Provisions, Henry III summoned his men to Oxford for 30 March, the first Sunday in Lent, and took their counsel. Three bishops excommunicated his enemies, and on Thursday 3 April he marched for Northampton, the dragon standard that spelt no quarter flying before him. The action that followed marked the war's legal beginning, the first deliberate act of open rebellion. Henry III's capture of Northampton on Saturday 5 April was a heavy blow for the rebels. The only military victory Henry ever won, it nearly ended the war at a stroke.

Thirteenth-century Northampton was a place of strategic and economic significance. Before the Fens were drained, the best route from southern England to the Midlands and North ran along the watershed that divides streams flowing east to the Wash from those flowing west into the Avon and the Bristol Channel. Forests and swamps restricted movement to the high ground across which the Romans ran Fosse Way and Watling Street, the main A5 road from Dover to Chester. Northampton lies just 8 miles (13km) north of Watling Street, on the river Nene's north bank, with links to Leicester, Peterborough, Bedford and Cirencester. Its Montfortian garrison protected Simon's own main area of support outside the capital, threatened Henry III's headquarters at Oxford, separated the king from his northern supporters and potentially could outflank royalist offensives towards London or the Severn Valley.

Northampton's central location made it a choice venue for parliaments, Church councils and tournaments; King John's barons besieged it in 1215 and William Marshal rallied his supporters there before Lincoln. Another battle was fought there in 1460 during the War of the Roses. The most

King Saul in 13th-century guise addresses his army: such forces could move with remarkable speed, despite carts loads of spare arms and luxuries for the chivalry. (The Pierpont Morgan Library, New York M638 f23r)

The Lewes Campaign, April–May 1264

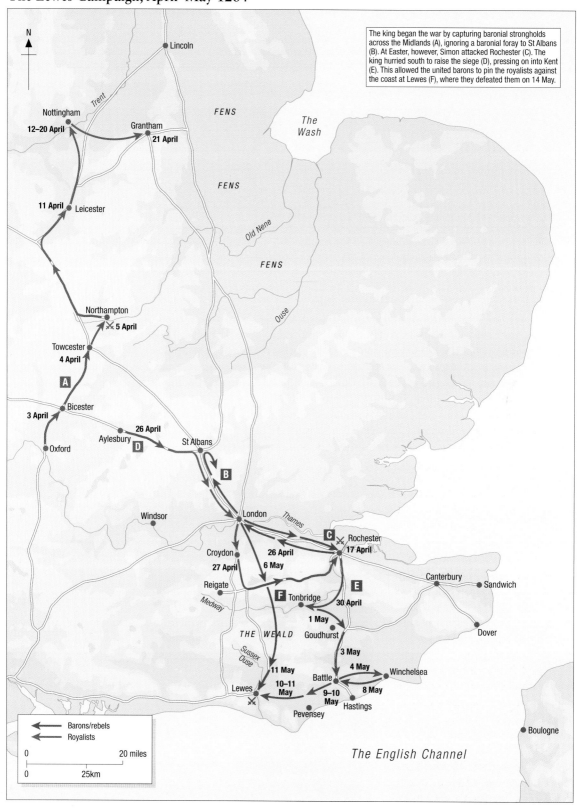

The king began the war by capturing baronial strongholds across the Midlands (A), ignoring a baronial foray to St Albans (B). At Easter, however, Simon attacked Rochester (C). The king hurried south to raise the siege (D), pressing on into Kent (E). This allowed the united barons to pin the royalists against the coast at Lewes (F), where they defeated them on 14 May.

N

Lincoln

FENS

The Wash

Nottingham
12–20 April

Grantham
21 April

Trent

FENS

11 April Leicester

FENS

Old Nene

Northampton
5 April

Ouse

Towcester
4 April

A

Bicester
3 April

26 April
Aylesbury D

St Albans

Oxford

B

Windsor

London Thames

C Rochester
17 April

Croydon

26 April
6 May

Canterbury Sandwich

27 April

Reigate

E

Medway

F Tonbridge
30 April

1 May

Dover

THE WEALD
Goudhurst

Sussex Ouse

3 May

4 May

Winchelsea

11 May
10–11 May

Battle

8 May

Lewes

9–10 May Hastings

Pevensey

Boulogne

Barons/rebels
Royalists

0   20 miles
0   25km

The English Channel

important Midland town of its day, Northampton was a royal borough with walls and a castle, since demolished to build the railway station. Its 13th-century population included some 300 cloth-workers. With their families, they might represent over 1,000 people engaged in that activity, when major cities such as Norwich had a population of 6,000. Simon de Montfort recognized Northampton's importance, placing a reliable man in command of the castle, and swearing the burgesses to his cause.

Northampton's accessibility made it vulnerable. Starting at Oxford, 40 miles (64km) to the south, Henry III could ride there in two days compared with the three Simon needed for the 64 miles (102km) from London. Henry had a day in hand to crush its defenders, without allowing time for news of his offensive to reach the capital. Henry's route was straightforward: north along Buckle Street, the Roman road that passes east of Oxford through Otmoor and Bicester, before intersecting Watling Street at Towcester. A royalist advanced party reached Northampton on the Friday evening and summoned the defenders to surrender, which they declined to do.

Several sources suggest the garrison expected to hold out until the older de Montfort could relieve them. Wykes says they underestimated royalist numbers. Except for their leaders, the younger Simon and Peter de Montfort, the rebels named in contemporary narratives appear to have been simple knights. They were unlikely to field so many retainers as grandees such as Richard of Cornwall or the Lord Edward. Wykes also states Henry had attracted many knights returning from the recent parliament at Windsor. Between 60 and 100 rebel knights were captured in the fighting, with an unknown number of rank and file. Besides them, the defenders fielded townsmen, fighting to defend their homes, and men-at-arms from the local *posse comitatus*, pressed into fighting the king.

Henry III was well acquainted with Northampton, and the course of the action suggests local knowledge. At sunrise on Saturday, about 5:40am, some royalists advanced over the water meadows south of the town to attack its main gate with 'engines', which might just mean ladders or hurdles. Meanwhile, another party rode clockwise along the built-up area's western perimeter, looking for an easier entrance. How far this was deliberate, or the natural response to a failed attack on the gate, is unknown. Rishanger implies premeditation, but he is a late source. Others disagree as to which party the king led, which might have provided a clue. If Henry led the turning movement, that was the main attack, the southern attack a diversion. While the townsmen entrusted with the southern sector held up the initial attack, the outflanking detachment found a breach 40 horses wide in the garden wall of St Andrew's Priory, at the north end of town.

Montfortian chroniclers claimed foul play. The Prior was a Poitevin, an obvious traitor. Rishanger explains at length how

The river Nene, looking north from the bridge in Grafton Street, towards the area where the royalists crossed the stream and broke into the Priory. A plaque in Grafton Street commemorates the Prior's treachery. (Photograph courtesy of Graham Evans)

the walls had been undermined 'with foxlike care', shored up with wooden props, and word sent to the king at Oxford. Even the reliable and contemporary Dunstable annalist believed it. Following Lewes, Simon's government would suspend the Prior, who was reinstated after Evesham. Wykes only says the attackers threw down part of the wall lightly – *leviter*. Royal correspondence, not available to chroniclers, suggests everyday dilapidation and public neglect. The walls were in a poor state. The king had remitted local taxes to the town for repairs, 'for his security and theirs'. The work does not seem to have been done. North of the castle, the river Nene was not much of an obstacle.

Young Simon reacted to the break-in in the proper chivalric manner, riding up on a foaming horse with his squire and an unknown sergeant to contest the breach. At the attackers' third onset 'he less wisely leapt into the breach in the wall, but his horse charged on, mindless of his master's safety, the reins hanging loose; spurred on vigorously, carrying away his unwilling rider, he contrived to fall into the ditch at the breach; and those outside not being slow to pull their illustrious captive out of the ditch nearly unhurt, he surrendered, not without relief, to the Lord Edward' (Wykes).

The war had yet to become the deadly affair it was at Evesham; so it remained a rough game played for ransoms and honour.

Simon's capture threw the defenders into disarray, 'thinking no more of their own defence or the town's, thrown into mental confusion, [they] were struck so motionless after this that they could no longer resist' (ibid.). Peter de Montfort escaped into the castle with a few men, but he was hopelessly outnumbered, and the castle's defences no better maintained than the town's. Official reports describe the western walls as near collapse, the turrets lacking roofs. Temporary wooden repairs had been ordered, but neither castle nor garrison were in any state for a siege.

Peter surrendered next day, the entire baronial army falling into enemy hands. One elderly knight is known to have died – Henry de Eyville, who preferred death to defeat. Contemporary estimates of knightly prisoners start at 60, running to 75, 80 or 85. Wykes's 'hundred or more' looks like propaganda. There were uncounted numbers of '*satellites*': squires, sergeants and burgesses. Rishanger described the haul as 'a great part of the barons' army', a major loss. Conversely, the royal cause was boosted by the demonstration of kingly power, and the wealth transferred from rebel prisoners to royal supporters as ransoms. Henry of Isham, captured by Henry III's crossbowmen, had to pay 40 marks, £26 13s. 4d. at two thirds of a pound to the mark.

Northampton's citizens suffered most, although there is no evidence of generalized slaughter. Leading citizens suffered fines rather than execution. The Dunstable annalist reports, 'those who were with the king, plundered the burgesses and everyone else to the last penny'. Even the royalist Wykes admitted the town was pillaged without mercy: 'The king's lords, drunk with victory, loaded with plunder, enriched with spoiling the prisoners, so that they might have fully satisfied the greed of their pockets, sparing neither sacred nor secular places, carrying off whatever they could find … left a most flourishing town in poverty, emptied of all its goods.'

Wykes may have exaggerated the sacrilege to explain the forthcoming disaster at Lewes. The only administrative evidence for damage to ecclesiastical property is a writ of February 1265, noting that St Andrew's

Priory was 'so deteriorated by occasion of the late conflict in the town … the discipline of the order cannot be maintained'. Confirmation that the Priory bore the brunt of the fighting, such damage is no evidence of treachery.

The victory's strategic effects were immediate. Within a week, the royal host took Leicester and Nottingham unopposed, despite the latter's unparalleled natural and artificial defences. The Lord Edward swept on to capture the dissident Earl Ferrars's castle at Tutbury, near Burton-on-Trent, wasting baronial property across Staffordshire and Derbyshire as he went. The Wirksworth area paid £200 to escape burning. This destructive *chevauchée* was no futile diversion. Edward could not know Ferrars would stand aloof from the decisive struggle in the south; it made sense to undermine his economic base. Royalist reinforcements poured in *vehementer*. The one bright spot for Midland rebels came when a party from Kenilworth prevented Warwick Castle's governor changing sides, pulling down the walls between the towers to deny its use to the enemy.

The older Simon had left London with a relief column of knights and citizen militia, believing that Northampton still held out. He learned of its fall at St Albans. Simultaneous news of a conspiracy to hand London over to the Lord Edward demanded an immediate return. Rishanger attributed the plot to the Jews who were alleged to have copied keys to the city gates, excavated tunnels and prepared Greek fire to burn the city. However improbable, this gave Simon's followers an excuse to massacre and plunder London's Jewish community. Traditionally royal property, they were vulnerable during civil wars, when debtors exploited the disorder to destroy evidence of their indebtedness. Similar disturbances occurred in 1215. Except for the Jews, however, the first round of the war had gone to the king.

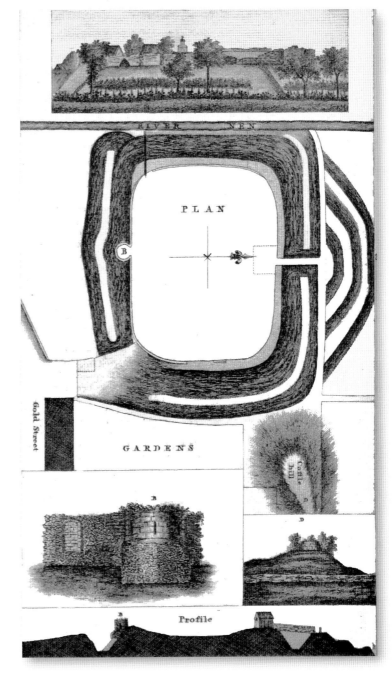

Northampton Castle drawn for the *Gentleman's Magazine* in 1800 – from top: the ruins seen from the west; plan view of the earthworks; the last remaining tower on the southern ramparts; Castle Hill; cross-section showing the depth of the ditch. (Author's collection)

Assault on Northampton, 5 April 1264

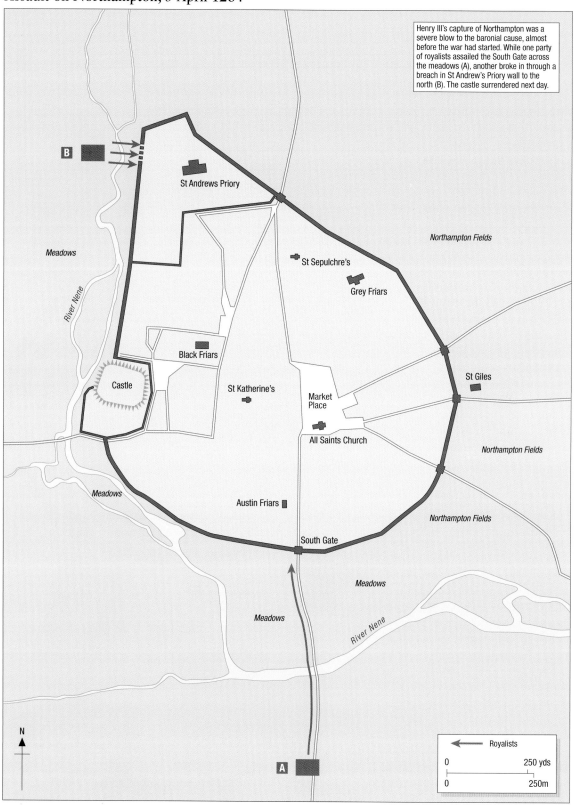

Henry III's capture of Northampton was a severe blow to the baronial cause, almost before the war had started. While one party of royalists assailed the South Gate across the meadows (A), another broke in through a breach in St Andrew's Priory wall to the north (B). The castle surrendered next day.

B

St Andrews Priory

Meadows

Northampton Fields

River Nene

St Sepulchre's

Grey Friars

Black Friars

Castle

St Katherine's

Market Place

St Giles

All Saints Church

Northampton Fields

Meadows

Austin Friars

Northampton Fields

South Gate

Meadows

Meadows

River Nene

N

A

Royalists

0   250 yds

0   250m

THE SIEGE OF ROCHESTER

The king's departure for the northern Midlands left the field open for Simon to regain the initiative in the south. Before leaving Oxford, Henry III had detached John de Warenne and Roger of Leyburne to Reigate and Rochester to safeguard his interests thereabouts against 'the irruptions of the Londoners' (Rishanger). Henry's absence left his southern lieutenants vulnerable to a coup-de-main. Of the two castles, Rochester was the more tempting. Halfway between Dover and London, it covered the ancient bridge where Watling Street crossed the river Medway. Its capture would consolidate the baronial grip on the south-east, and hinder the passage of any foreign mercenaries the exiled Queen might send over from her refuge in France. Conveniently placed, near the Earl of Gloucester's castle at Tonbridge, it was accessible by water, facilitating the transport of siege material. Besides, its garrison was implicated in the plot to set London ablaze with Greek fire.

Like Northampton, Rochester was a strategic sore point. William Rufus besieged it in 1087, and King John did so again in 1215. Its fortifications were appropriately strong. Diamond shaped, the defences were oriented to the main compass points, the bailey surrounded by deep ditches and crenellated stone walls on an earth bank. The keep was in the southern corner, its 12ft-thick walls (3.6m) strengthened by corner towers. One of these had been cylindrical since 1215, when King John's miners brought it down. Its capture had cost him 51 days and his entire war-chest of £40,000. Simon would need all his warrior skills to take Rochester in the week at his disposal.

Baronial forces appeared either side of the Medway on Maundy Thursday, 17 April. Wykes makes a great fuss about the impiety of fighting in Holy Week, but it was the pious Henry III who began the war in Lent, a traditional close season for military activity. Coming from Tonbridge, Gloucester invested the town's landward side, supported by the baronial garrison from

Rochester Castle and Cathedral from the Medway in the 1890s: the Medway was a major obstacle, requiring a full-scale amphibious assault. Simon's ships were probably no larger than Victorian barges. (Author's collection)

Dover. He had the usual 'large army' with several diehard Montfortians who reappear at Lewes and Evesham: John fitzJohn, Henry Hastings and Nicholas Seagrave, 'with many other nobles and many commons' (Canterbury). Simon and the Londoners were over the river at Strood, having marched down the main road from the capital.

The defenders included both of Henry's local commanders, besides 'many other knights and a numerous garrison'. The word 'many' needs qualification. Official figures for Angevin garrisons in the previous century suggest an average of 115 fighting men. Henry III's Regent hanged all 83 of Bedford Castle's garrison after a major siege in 1224, sparing only the chaplain and three Templars. Estimates of Rochester's garrison during King John's siege are about average: 100–140. A similar figure appears likely in 1264. Besides the official garrison, the townspeople also participated in the defence. The garrison had no intention of giving in. Before Gloucester could shut them up inside, Roger of Leyburne sallied forth and burnt all the suburbs along the road to Canterbury, besides a great part of the town and priory. This was common practice to deny attackers shelter from weather and missiles. When William Marshal invested Newark Castle in 1218, his knights had rushed the town to forestall its defenders' firing the houses.

Today the Medway is 200–500 yards wide below Rochester and over 20ft deep, although it was probably wider and shallower in the 13th century. The Romans had forced their way across in AD 43 with catapults and specialist bridging equipment. Like them, Simon came prepared: 'a careful man in everything, he ordered from the city of London in advance the engines and other requisites for the capture of a castle to be taken round with him by water and land, with which he violently attacked the defenders, nor allowed them any peace (Rishanger).'

The citizens, anxious to avoid Northampton's fate, had broken down part of the bridge, and fortified their own end with a wooden gatehouse. After they had twice repulsed his men, Simon launched an amphibious assault with a fire-ship, 'setting an example for the English, of how the assault of a castle should be carried out, which previously to those days, was unknown to them' (ibid.). Again, this needs qualification. The siege of Bedford had been a model of remorseless pressure. That was four decades earlier, however. Its organizers, veterans of King John's wars, were long gone.

Crusaders armed with bows, staff slings and ladders storm Damietta on the Nile. Simon's amphibious assault on Rochester will have used similar techniques. (Matthew Paris MS 16 59v by kind permission of the Master and Fellows of Corpus Christi College Cambridge)

Rishanger simply says that Simon had a boat piled up with dry wood, covered with fat, grease and other inflammable material; the more local Canterbury chronicle specifies pitch, sulphur and charcoal as well as pig fat. The mixture lies midway between the 'forty bacon pigs of the fattest and less good sort for eating' with which King John fired his mines at Rochester, and the gunpowder described by Grosseteste's pupil Roger Bacon. Towards evening on Good Friday, 18 April, having stationed the boat upwind and set fire to its contents, the rebels drifted her down against the bridge, covered by a barrage of arrows and crossbow bolts from the far bank to stop the defenders fending her off.

Simon followed in further craft with his own men and the Londoners, driving the burgesses from the blazing gatehouse. The casualty list betrays the small scale of the operation, four or five townsmen killed, according to the Dunstable annalist. Another source confirms that Simon's landing party was but few. Next day, Saturday the 19th, the attackers pressed their advantage. Deploying engines and catapults, they stormed the bailey, something that took King John several weeks, and shut the defenders up within the keep. Casualties were rising, including Roger of Leyburne who was roughly handled. Fighting resumed on Monday, after a pause for Easter Sunday, but the defenders repelled all further attacks, despite machines battering their walls, and miners digging underneath.

The rebels had no time to spring their mine. The following Saturday, 26 April, reports came that relief was close at hand, and seditious spirits were plotting to surrender London to the Lord Edward. Walter of Guisborough records one of the few scraps of strategic debate to survive from this period. Simon's advisers were nervous of losing the base that guaranteed their freedom of manoeuvre: 'If the king occupies London by his advance, we shall be bottled up here, as if in a corner of the land. Let us go back to London, therefore, so we may save both the place and the people'. In the silence of the night Simon withdrew most of his forces, *noctis silentio* as Wykes put it, leaving a party to hold the siege lines. The Londoners returned to the capital,

The keep at Rochester Castle from the point of view of Simon de Montfort's men in the outer bailey, showing the close quarters required for siege warfare. Unlike King John, Simon failed to get in. (Postcard from author's collection)

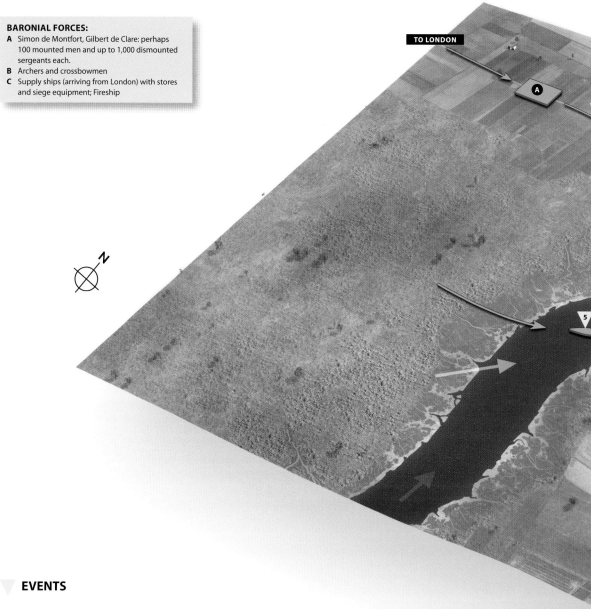

BARONIAL FORCES:
A Simon de Montfort, Gilbert de Clare: perhaps 100 mounted men and up to 1,000 dismounted sergeants each.
B Archers and crossbowmen
C Supply ships (arriving from London) with stores and siege equipment; Fireship

▼ **EVENTS**

1 Baronial pincer movement on Rochester from the north and south.

2 Royalist sortie to burn suburbs to deprive the besiegers of cover.

3 Simon's abortive attack on the bridge (morning 18 April).

4 Baronial missile troops bombard bridge defenders.

5 Simon's amphibious assault to take south end of the bridge (evening 18 April).

6 Baronial follow-up drives the royalists into keep (19 April).

7 Gilbert's advance against the cathedral to complete the investment.

ASSAULT ON ROCHESTER, 17–19 APRIL 1264

Baronial forces beset Rochester from two directions on 17 April (1), the garrison firing the suburbs (2). Initial assaults on the bridge next morning were repulsed (3). That evening, however, supported by archers shooting across the river (4), Simon launched an amphibious assault, wind and current carrying his fireship across to fire the bridge defences (5). Next morning he captured the castle's outer bailey, the garrison retiring inside the keep (6). Meanwhile, Gilbert de Clare took the cathedral (7). The siege then bogged down, a royalist relief force (not shown) forcing them to withdraw on 26 April.

Note: Gridlines are shown at intervals of 500m

ROYALIST FORCES
1   Castle garrison: perhaps a score of knights and 100 sergeants.
2   A few score townsmen defending the bridge.

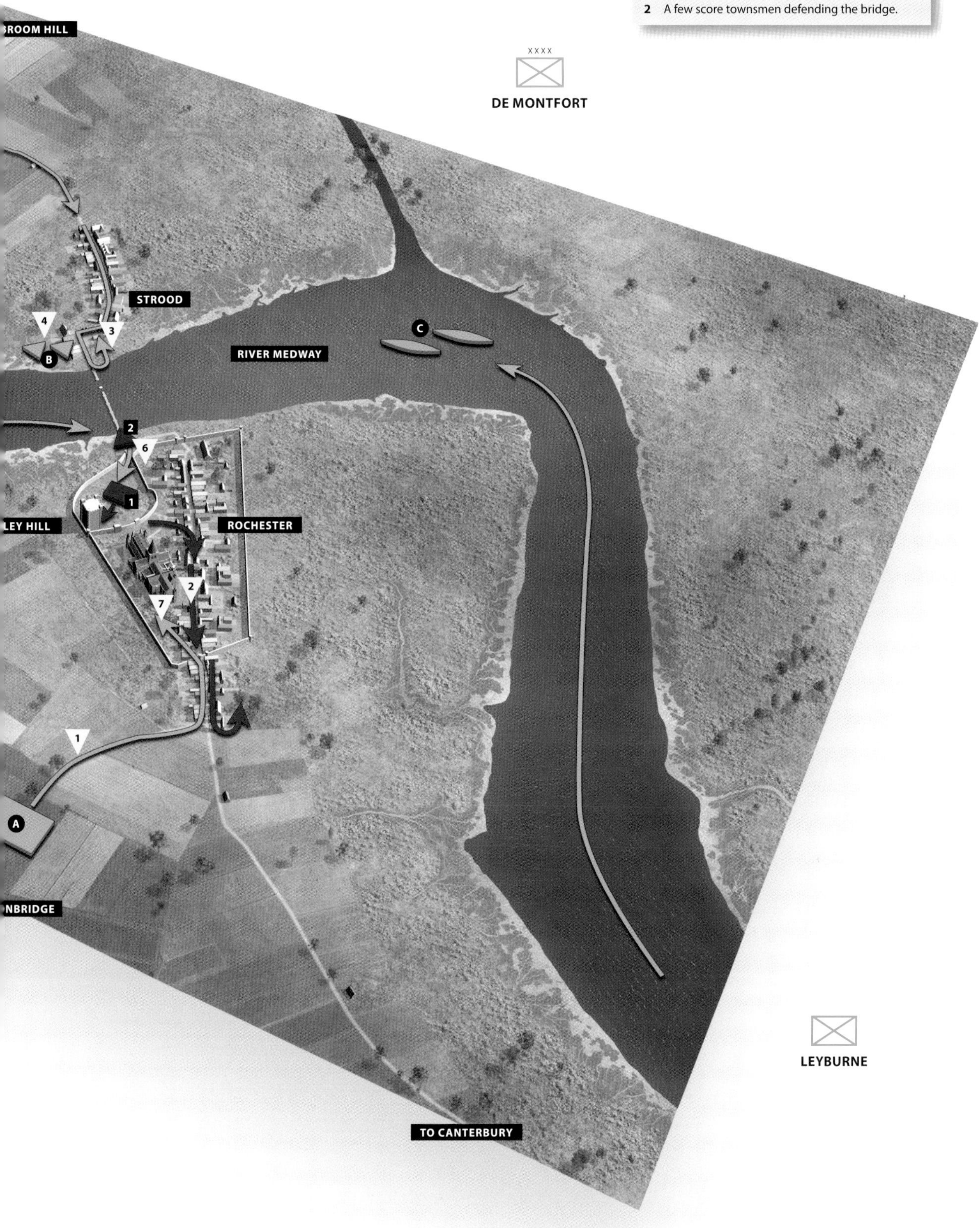

xxxx
DE MONTFORT

BROOM HILL

STROOD

RIVER MEDWAY

ROCHESTER

LEY HILL

NBRIDGE

LEYBURNE

TO CANTERBURY

33

the two earls to Tonbridge, in case Edward came that way. Several commentators claimed that, given another day or two, the castle must have fallen. This looks optimistic. The average siege lasted 38 days; Simon had just ten.

Henry III was celebrating Easter at Nottingham when news came that Rochester was under fierce attack. Any castle must fall if not relieved, the garrison's capture casting inevitable discredit upon their lord. The relief of a place under siege was a well-established way of bringing an unwilling besieger to battle. Simon's father had done so at Muret and the Marshal at Lincoln. The recent arrival at Nottingham of Henry's northern supporters, with 'many thousand men-at-arms', had increased the king's numerical advantage. He might feel confident of the outcome of any accidental confrontation.

Once more, Henry's alacrity belied his dilatory reputation. On Easter Sunday, he marched to Grantham on Ermine Street, the main London road from the north. Contemporary chroniclers with little basis for comparison thought his speed unprecedented, but, as discussed above, their claims are exaggerated. Nevertheless, Henry was at Aylesbury by Friday 25 April, a day's hard riding from London. As in 1216, the citizens came forth in arms to confront an unpopular king, and he turned aside to Kingston-upon-Thames. Advanced elements reached Croydon the same day. This advance placed the royalists on internal lines again, threatening London or Rochester. Simon had to choose between his base and his prey. When he withdrew to cover the capital, the royalists doubled back to take Kingston Castle before pressing on to Rochester on the 28th. Noticing Simon's departure, the garrison had already launched a dawn raid and caught his rearguard, abandoned as sacrificial victims said Wykes, cutting off their hands and feet. It must have seemed as if Simon had been wrong-footed again. He had succeeded in drawing the royal army away from his allies in the Midlands, but failed to take Rochester. Meanwhile, two more castles had been lost; Tonbridge fell on 1 May, its castellan firing the town in the customary manner. Once more the initiative lay with the king.

The Earl of Gloucester's castle at Tonbridge refashioned as a country house: few rebel castles held out long against the royal host. Tonbridge fell on 1 May 'without any trouble'. (Postcard from author's collection)

THE KING'S MARCH TO LEWES

The siege of Rochester confirmed the rebels' inability to confront the king's undivided forces in the field. As long as they controlled London, however, and kept their own army in being, they posed a threat. Great cities were almost impossible to besiege, especially when built on a major river like London. Louis VII of France failed to invest Rouen in 1174, the citizens bringing in supplies across the river Seine. The Norman capital only fell to the French in 1204 because King John lacked the political will to defend it. When London held out after William Marshal's stunning victories at Lincoln and Sandwich, he ended the First Barons' War by negotiation rather than run the political and economic risks of storming England's chief commercial entrepôt. Henry III later criticized his Regent's choice, but he was no more anxious to confront the Londoners on their home ground.

Henry marched south from Tonbridge towards the Kent coast, 'as if glorying in his triumph' (Wykes). The chronicler did not know who suggested the move, but he knew its purpose. Like Marshal after Sandwich, Henry needed the shipping to blockade London. He was making for the Cinque Ports, 'so he might persuade them from love or compel them by fear to attack London with a piratical fleet, or at all events block up their trade, so the great mass of shipping might not sail up there with supplies.' Presumably Henry followed the Roman road south to Hastings, the confederacy's westernmost town, avoiding the rebel garrison at Dover. The Cinque Ports had been maritime guardians of the Channel since before the Norman Conquest, their hegemony based on piracy and fishing rather than trade. They had a tradition of opposition to the Crown. King John lost their support, facilitating the French invasion of 1216–17. William Marshal purchased their renewed loyalty with bribes and promises to respect their ancient liberties. They were essential partners in any attempt to apply maritime pressure on London, hence Henry's wish 'to bind them more tightly to himself, since they were visibly not amenable to his will' (Waverley).

The undeveloped woodlands between Tonbridge and Hastings were a challenge for any army. Supplies were scarce; its free population resented intruders. Thomas Wykes's account of

Kentish archers harassed the royalists in the Weald, but the weapon was widespread. This northern example appears on the West Porch at Lincoln Cathedral. Note the string pulled to the ear, as shown by Matthew Paris. (Author's photograph)

the siege of Rochester is brief and rhetorical. His circumstantial evocation of royalist tribulations on the march south suggests his informant took part, perhaps as a member of Richard of Cornwall's household:

> The king's army could not march freely through the hilly counties of Surrey and Kent, for the Wealden archers bravely held them up in the narrow lanes, shooting arrows from a distance. But the unprotected bowmen attacked the armoured soldiers in vain. On capture they were beheaded by the king's men as fitting punishment. While the king remained in this unproductive region with his innumerable army, many wasted away for lack of food, fainting from excessive hunger, transport animals bellowed and broke down for want of fodder.

On the first day, 2 May, someone shot the king's cook at Goudhurst, and 300 local archers were beheaded in reprisal. Next day Henry reached Battle Abbey, near Hastings, which he fined 100 marks (£67) for their tenants' disloyalty. On the 4th the host struck east to Winchelsea, where Henry received the men of the Cinque Ports into his peace and took hostages for their good behaviour. Rishanger claimed the mariners sailed away, as their ancestors did when menaced by the French in 1217, leaving Henry and his hungry men to console themselves with the contents of the wine merchants' cellars.

Lewes Castle's most impressive angle, showing its massive southern mound and the shell keep's surviving masonry with octagonal enfilading towers, a recent addition in 1264: a secure refuge for a king. (Author's photograph)

The repulse at Rochester, after previous setbacks, inspired intense debate in London: not just among baronial leaders, but across the social spectrum, clerical and lay. The Furness Chronicle suggests that, seeing themselves weaker than the king, they sought peace, offering compensation for their depredations, but Henry's counsellors rebuffed their advances. Rishanger says the barons prepared to fight, so 'they might try, having given battle in

LEWES CASTLE

the open field, on whom fate might be seen to confer victory'. Men poured in to join the Earl's army, 15,000 Londoners besides countless others from all sides. These must have included survivors of the royalists' Midland campaign as both Henry de Montfort and John Giffard, fresh from slighting Warwick Castle, fought at Lewes. On 6 May, Simon left London to seek battle.

Henry's march into the Weald's distant thickets had altered the strategic balance to his disadvantage. He left a significant garrison at Tonbridge to cover his rear: over 20 banners, 200–400 mounted men, perhaps a quarter of his cavalry. The royal host diminished and removed to a safe distance, the rebels regained freedom of movement. Back at Battle Abbey on Friday 9 May, Henry heard Simon had left London and was on his track. The royalists had planned to march on Canterbury, whence they could operate against London or Dover with their seaborne allies. Now they scrambled to find a secure refuge for the king, the main piece on the board, who now rode in his armour to frustrate snipers. Marching west through Hurstmonceux, skirting the Pevensey Levels, they reached Lewes's shelter on 10 or 11 May. Chronological uncertainty may imply haste, or just poor march discipline over bad roads. Simon appeared the next day, 'two days before the battle', sheltering his army in the woods around Fletching. Nine miles (14km) north of Lewes, blocking the road north, Fletching was an awkward position to attack with an army such as Henry's that was built around mounted troops. The stage was set for the campaign's bloody denouement. Hemmed in between Downs and Channel, Henry could not avoid a battle if Simon wanted one.

LEWES AND ITS SURROUNDINGS

The county town of East Sussex owes its pre-eminence to the gap it occupies in the South Downs through which the Sussex Ouse finds its way to the sea. River and road traffic intersect, making the town a commercial and strategic centre. Anglo-Saxon Lewes was a royal borough with a market and two mints. In 1217

Lewes town and castle from the Downs, looking towards Cliffe Hill from the traditional battle site at Landport Bottom. Note the steep drop towards Walland Park, centre left. (Author's photograph)

it saw a French column ambushed by local resistance fighters. Six miles (10km) inland, the river is tidal. In the 13th century, the Ouse still flooded the reclaimed area south of Lewes known as The Brooks. The priory's charter refers to several nearby hills as islands. Lewes High Street, the town's backbone, runs west to east along a spur 100ft above sea-level. This tongue of high ground falls away on all sides except the west, the river looping around its eastern end to divide Lewes from its suburb at Cliffe. A bridge replacing a Roman ford joined the two settlements. North of Lewes, the Ouse runs north-west, hugging the Downs, creating a narrow defile which restricts access to the town from the north.

High ground encloses the town on both sides. Cliffe Hill rises steeply to 539ft (164m) on the east. The hill to the west, where the fighting took place, climbs more gently to 639ft (195m) at Mount Harry, just over 2 miles (4km) north-west of Lewes Castle. In 1264 the Downs were common land, grazed by sheep, whose nibbling kept the slopes clear. Today thorn bushes, rowan and sycamore channel movement onto the spur along a narrow chalk track, which once crossed open grassland. Higher up, on top of the Downs, the ground is more open. Once a race course, it slopes up across the Ordnance Survey's marked battlefield site at Landport Bottom, culminating at Offham Hill on the right and Mount Harry on the left. North of these heights, the ground falls away abruptly to Combe Place and Hamsey (83ft), providing observation towards the rebel encampment at Fletching and south into Lewes itself. The advantages of such a dominant position for modern armies possessing long-range weaponry are clear. They are less so for a medieval army denied weapons effective beyond 250 yards. Narrow and precipitous paths lead up the northern escarpment at Offham and Blackcap, half a mile beyond Mount Harry (800m).

Lewes town lacked stone walls at the time of the battle. The first grant of *murage* dates from 1266, presumably in reaction to recent events. The walls, when built, enclosed a triangular perimeter, probably following an earlier earth bank and palisade, traces of which remain either side of Westgate. The space within measures 550 yards (500m) along the High Street, and 495 yards (450m) from its eastern apex to the middle of its base at Mount Brack, the northernmost of the castle's two mounds. Domesday Book recorded 385 households in Lewes, suggesting a population of nearly 2,000. This might have doubled or trebled by 1264.

Lewes Castle from the north-west before housing obscured the artificially scarped slope protecting its northern perimeter. The two mottes are separated by an extensive inner bailey. (Original watercolour courtesy of Eileen Brooks)

The town's main defence was its castle, north-west of the High Street. Lewes is almost unique among English castles in having two conical earth mounds or mottes, both surrounded by dry ditches. The other example is at Lincoln. The higher south-westerly mound is capped by the remains of a shell keep, 65ft above the High Street, with stone walls 10ft thick. About half of these survive, complete with enfilading towers added earlier in the 13th century. The lower summit of Mount Brack, 200 yards to the north-east, is innocent of masonry, although a 17th-century map shows a shell keep. Between the mounds lay the bailey, an oval space some 150 by 130 yards, once containing domestic buildings, such as stables and kitchens. Like Lincoln, the bailey could accommodate a significant force by medieval standards.

The southern motte at Lewes Castle from the barbican. The rear wall's absence reveals the limited space enclosed by the shell keep at the top of the mound. The zig-zag path is modern. (Author's photograph)

An existing slope improved by scarping protects the bailey's northern side, falling to the Paddock and Hangman's Acre. Along the more vulnerable south side a strong earth bank is still partly visible, lined with a stone rampart. The castle's most striking feature post-dates the battle. The impressive Barbican, leading to the High Street, was built in front of the old gatehouse, again in response to the fighting. One archway of the earlier Norman structure remains, with some scraps of the south curtain. In 1264, the castle was held by John de Warenne, descended from one of William the Conqueror's closest associates. John's loyalty, demonstrated by his recent defence of Rochester, combined with his castle's remarkable defences, made Lewes an attractive refuge.

Half a mile further south lay another great medieval structure, Lewes Priory. Founded by the Conqueror's companion William de Warenne, its walls enclosed some 32 acres, more spacious quarters than the castle. While the Lord Edward roughed it there with his companions, the two kings lodged within the monastic precincts.

Much of Lewes Priory has been destroyed. The remaining accommodation, the ruined dormitory shown here and the refectory, suggest there was ample space for King Henry and his retinue. (Author's photograph)

Protestantism and the railway have swept away the Great Church that dominated the priory, but the monks' ruined Infirmary and Dormitory suggest the scale of the accommodation. Besides suiting Henry III's religious pre-occupations, the priory was a secure location for royal headquarters, covered to the north by town and castle, to the south by tidal swamps.

Lewes Castle's most impressive feature is the Barbican, built after the battle. Behind it stands the front wall of the Norman gatehouse, attacked during the battle, and part of the curtain wall. (Author's photograph)

Access to the priory was via a gatehouse to the north, abutting the parish church of Southover, a settlement that occupied the ridge between the priory and a stream known as the Winterbourne. Dry in summer, this runs eastwards into the Ouse from the foot of the Downs. North of the Winterbourne, these extended right up to the edge of town, an uninterrupted grassy sward surrounding its western side. Troops leaving Lewes through the Westgate, next to the still extant Bull House, found themselves immediately on the Downs. A similarly open prospect met the king's men as they left the priory, an easy half mile march from Southover across the now built-up area known as the Hides, as far as the gentle upwards slope past the site of the present prison.

In the Middle Ages, three significant structures punctuated the line of what is now Western Road, which runs along the spur the eastern extremity of which the town centre occupies: St Anne's Church at its highest point (originally St Mary's); Snelling's Mill shown on a 1618 map near the Black Horse public house; St Nicholas's leper hospital in Spital Road, now a community centre. Several mills feature in reconstructions of the battle, in particular one near point 186 on the old Ordnance Survey one-inch map above the prison.

Either side of Western Road the ground falls steeply away, limiting the frontage of an army leaving Lewes by that route. Now obscured by housing, the useable space available is not much more than 500 yards. Accounts of the battle do not always acknowledge the constraints this placed upon the royal army. Just short of the prison, Spital Road, Western Road's continuation, crosses Nevill Road (the A275), before continuing up the second of three spurs likened to splayed fingers. These have dominated discussion of the battle: the westernmost between Ashcombe House and Houndean Bottom; the middle one at the prison; the northernmost from Landport Bottom to Nevill Road. It will be argued below that only the second middle one saw any fighting.

PRELUDE TO BATTLE

If Simon de Montfort made directly for Lewes along the Roman road that crosses the North Downs near Biggin Hill, he only needed to march a leisurely 7½ miles (12km) a day to arrive on the same day as Henry III. If he went via Tonbridge, as A. H. Burne suggested, before doubling back to the Roman road at Edenbridge, the daily march rate rises to 10 miles (16km), well within the capacity of his infantry. The latter course makes sense, menacing the royalists about Hastings while enabling the baronial army to pick up the Earl of Gloucester, rumoured to be hovering near Tonbridge.

Monday and Tuesday, 12–13 May, were spent in diplomatic, tactical and spiritual preparations for battle. Even at this late stage, the rebels simulated

Lewes: approach to battle, 13–14 May 1264

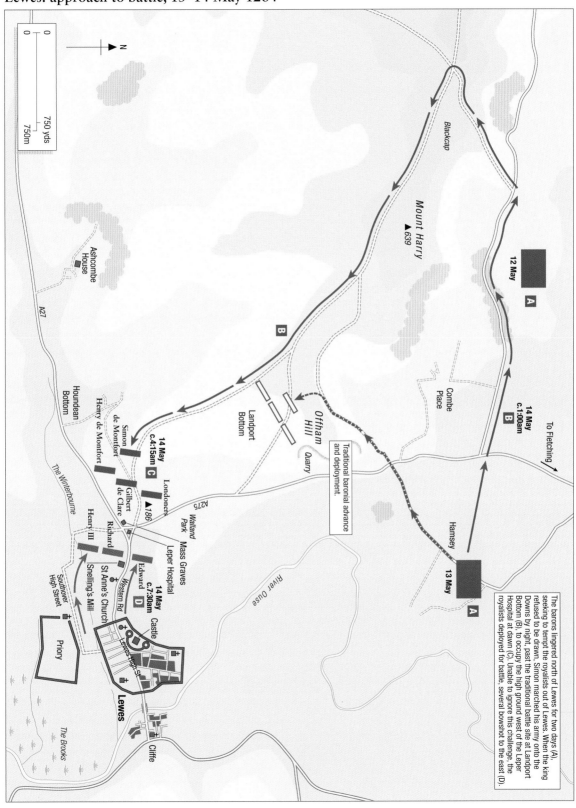

The barons lingered north of Lewes for two days (A), seeking to tempt the royalists out of Lewes. When the king refused to be drawn, Simon marched his army onto the Downs by night, past the traditional battle site at Landport Bottom (B), to occupy the high ground west of the Leper Hospital at dawn (C). Unable to ignore this challenge, the royalists deployed for battle, several bowshot to the east (D).

hopes for a peaceful settlement. On the Monday they proposed a deal based on the Provisions, subject to ecclesiastical arbitration, sweetened by 50,000 marks compensation (£33,333). Edward and Richard of Cornwall rejected the offer, 'suspecting the manifest disinheritance of the King of England, his brother, and their heirs, effectively threatening the reduction of their power' (Wykes). Having demonstrated the gulf between the parties, the rebels sent a letter of defiance the next day, protesting their personal loyalty to the king, while threatening 'our enemies who are also yours'. Henry VI's Yorkist opponents would employ a similar formula during the Wars of the Roses. Henry III rejected such sophistry, 'trusting in the mass of his supporters, and despising the fewness of the opposition party' (Wykes). Henry had been uniformly successful to date; he had no reason to back down now: 'writing back without greetings [a grave discourtesy], the king stated that he cared nothing for their service, but that he considered them his foes, and denounced them as public enemies. In addition, Edward the king's eldest and his uncle Richard … announced that they would destroy their and their men's goods, and also their bodies' (Waverley). The rebels in turn denounced their own homage and fealty. The last formal barriers to armed confrontation had been breached.

Under cover of these diplomatic manoeuvres, the rebels launched tactical probing initiatives north of Lewes, either seeking battle or a way onto the Downs. On the Monday, according to an under-utilized source known as the Gilson fragment, named after its Victorian editor, 'some who were with the Earl of Leicester appeared near Lewes'. The royal army advanced to the summit, and observed the enemy below, near some woods. More precisely, the royalists were up on Mount Harry, the rebels down in the pasture in front of the belt of woodland that extends westwards between the Downs and Warningore Wood to the north. The king, or his advisers, would not come down and fight. About lunchtime they rode back to Lewes.

Next day, his overtures rejected, Simon moved 'nearer Lewes than before', hoping 'to provoke the king's army to battle'. This was presumably opposite the northern end of the Offham defile, Simon's final letter of defiance being dated 'from the wood by Lewes'. Again, the royalist high command refused to fight at a disadvantage, as they would have to defile through the narrow space between the banks of the Ouse and the slope of the Downs. Simon may have hoped lack of supplies would compel his opponents to seek an early decision. British Army guidelines of 1914 estimated that a civilian population could subsist twice its own numbers for a week. A royal host approaching that ratio had been quartered upon Lewes for several days already. More than one source suggests their battle-winning destriers were already feeling the lack of forage.

The royalist aversion to tactical risk forced the rebels to take the bull by the horns. Their only rational option was a right flanking move onto the Downs west of Lewes, preferably by night to escape observation by royalist scouts on Mount Harry. A

Mount Harry from Offham Hill: the baronial army probably marched over the high ground in the distance, and advanced towards the camera, skirting the woods, before wheeling right (our left) to form line. (Author's photograph)

frontal advance straight down the Offham defile would allow the royalists to assail the head of the rebel column as it emerged close to Lewes Castle. A left flanking move across the Ouse to Cliffe was both difficult and pointless.

A night approach march is a risky undertaking. The Londoners spent all night preparing their weapons. Simon never slept, urging his companions by word and example to confess their sins and seek absolution so that 'cleansed in spirit from all defilement of sin, they might go boldly into battle, the more certain of a victory in which God was engaged' (Rishanger). Such spiritual exercises were usual before battle, either to promote a favourable outcome or as insurance against the opposite. More than one contemporary describes the battle of Lewes in religious terms: 'the Earl of Leicester with his men, having God and righteousness before their eyes, choosing rather to die for the truth, than break their sworn oath' (Dunstable). The royal army at Lincoln in 1217 had been similarly elevated, newly shriven, riding to victory or salvation. Like the Marshal's men, Simon's wore white crosses front and back. Helpful for distinguishing friend from foe, where both sides were using similar heraldic devices, these were also the traditional badge of English crusaders. Before starting, Simon, the most experienced leader present, allocated his unregimented troops to the ad hoc units in which they would fight: 'every man assigned to his banner, and each to his battle, according to military discipline, the order of advance and manner of attack to be taken from the field commander [i.e. Simon]' (Rishanger).

Rishanger thought this occurred outside Fletching. He is a remote authority, however, writing in about 1312. There seems no good reason to assume the rebel army returned there after its coat-trailing on the 13th. It seems more likely that, on the Monday evening, the rebels awaited their rations in the woods near the main road. They would, therefore, have started their march fresher and nearer their objective than usually supposed. One element in their favour was the moon, which the NASA moon phase database tells us was full at 7:51pm on the 12th.

Most commentators assume the rebels took the direct route up the north-east corner of the Downs from Combe. The Gilson fragment, however, states, 'the army of the barons came to Boxholte, which place is two leagues distant from Lewes'. A 1772 map shows Boxholte on the northern edge of the Downs, almost 2 miles (3km) west of Offham and 3 miles (5km) north-west of Lewes, a distance compatible with the chronicler's imprecise terminology. An ancient trackway runs directly from Boxholte to Blackcap, where the path tends to the right, *de dextrario* John of Oxnead styled it, towards Mount Harry. Here the rebels could draw breath, while the column closed up.

This indirect approach would bypass royalist patrols, while the further from Lewes the rebels could form line the better. Five hundred mounted men and 4,000 foot in column of twos for the narrow ascent, would extend some 6,000 yards in depth, just over 3 miles (5km). Moving at 2 miles an hour (3km/h), a conservative rate in the dark, it would take an hour and a half to close up, during which time they would not want to meet the enemy. A larger force would take longer, especially as medieval soldiers were not taught to march in step. The 3 miles from their starting point, assuming this was somewhere near Hamsey on the main road, would require another hour and a half. Sunrise in mid-May is about 4:15am. Simon would have needed to move off about 1:00am to reach Mount Harry just before dawn, which Rishanger says was the plan.

THE BATTLEFIELD

Rishanger did not say what Simon meant to do next. It is one thing to seize a dominant position by a bold coup-de-main; it is another to convert topographical advantage into tactical success. We do not know how Simon intended to develop his battle. Traditional 20th-century accounts, which remain the dominant narrative, imply he had nothing much in mind. Having captured a sleepy sentry on Mount Harry, the great Earl stopped at Landport Bottom, drew up his army across the south-east track of the future race course and knighted his younger followers. After working his army into a frenzy, and risking everything on a night march, the man who frightened Henry III more than thunder and lightning is supposed to have quietly handed the initiative back to the enemy.

Psychologically unconvincing, this idea is contradicted by a range of evidence. The battle's earliest students, including Oman and Barrett, followed the trail-blazing W. H. de Blaauw in locating the action at the foot of the Downs, 'in the close vicinity of the Lewes County Gaol, and … from thence to the walls of the town at Westgate, and to the walls of the priory gateway'. They could claim contemporary support. Thomas Wykes wrote: 'having unfurled their banners on the slope of a certain hill which lies *next* to Lewes town, where the king was then anxiously lying … they *came down* led by the earl' (author's emphases). John of Oxnead uses similar language. Westminster Abbey's *Flowers of History* mentions the king riding uphill, but then explains he never got up, being pre-empted by the rebels, '*coming down* the slope of the hill'.

Subsequently, the battlefield has migrated to the top of Downs, thanks to A. H. Burne's promoting the area for aesthetic reasons as a natural parade ground. There it remains, despite Professor Carpenter's comprehensive demolition of the idea in 1987. Unlike Burne, Carpenter based his arguments upon a thorough examination of all relevant sources. The Gilson fragment, which Burne used for his cursory estimate of the numbers engaged but not their location, describes the rebels advancing gingerly from Boxholte: 'at a slow step, having formed into divisions, to the mill which is *outside the house of the Lewes lepers*, and there the king came to meet them'. The moderate pace is convincing: knights advancing to contact were advised to ride as gently as if they were carrying a bride, to preserve their formation. The leper hospital was St Nicholas's in Spital Road. Now facing the prison, it was then opposite the unobstructed slope of the Downs. A manuscript at Trinity College Cambridge, linked to Gilbert de Clare who commanded Simon's central division, specifies the distance from Lewes as half a league. A 'league' might signify 1 or 3 miles. If the scribe meant the former, the battle occurred right by the prison.

Two other sources associate the battlefield with a mill. The *London Chronicle* refers to the barons moving 'towards a certain mill near Lewes against the king, whom they saw come with his army against them'. A helpful

Looking across the old racecourse towards the traditional battle site at Landport Bottom. Nestling in the re-entrant, the houses of Nevill Crescent show the steep slope that would have faced a royalist attack from that direction. (Author's photograph)

18th-century comment in the margin adds that this was 'called King Harry's mill to this day'. A.H. Burne's map shows this on the hill above the prison, but the mill there was not built until 300 years after the battle. Lewes Priory's own chronicle places the fighting somewhat mysteriously at the mill 'suellingi', apparently an ancient Kentish unit of land measurement. A more helpful reading is *ad molinendum snellingi*, 'at Snelling's Mill'. 'U' and 'n' were indistinguishable in medieval script, while Snelling was a local personal name. Tudor and Stuart references suggest that Snelling's and King Harry's Mill both stood in Western Road, between the hospital and St Anne's Church. Approaching from the west, the Gilson fragment's rebel source would naturally relate the mill to the structure nearest him, the hospital.

Physical confirmation of fighting at the foot of the Downs turned up in 1810 during construction of the prison. Three large pits were found at the jail's eastern carriage entrance while lowering the Brighton turnpike, near the junction of the modern A275 and A27 roads. The surveyor estimated that each pit contained 500 skeletons, a number far exceeding the number found anywhere else in the area. A. H. Burne claimed they had been removed from his favoured site, contradicting his own rule of thumb that mass graves always mark the hottest fighting. He did not explain why anyone should bother transporting 200 cart loads of mangled corpses a mile downhill. It seems unlikely they were victims of a prolonged pursuit. The most deadly moment of a medieval battle comes when the losers turn to flee, exposing their backs to the enemy. The winners, on the other hand, lose relatively few. It seems incontrovertible that the grave pits mark the spot where the defeated royalist infantry were cut down as they broke contact.

Lewes Prison and the Downs, seen from Lewes Castle, showing the height advantage enjoyed by troops occupying the slopes: the royalists probably formed up between St Anne's Church, spire extreme left, and the prison, left of centre. (Author's photograph)

A final topographical point tells in favour of the lower battle site. Everyone agrees the rebels were outnumbered, without explaining how they defeated larger numbers of similarly trained and equipped opponents. Medieval commentators sought spiritual explanations; modern materialists want something more tangible. The most plausible explanation is the slope down which the rebels charged towards the royalists advancing from the hospital. The Downs sky-line, as clearly visible from the castle's motte, hardly slopes at all. A French contemporary celebrated Simon as 'a valiant noble, [the] wisest man of the century', regarding him as a fellow countryman. He would hardly deserve such ardent praise had he idly thrown away the one material advantage that his hazardous night march had placed within his grasp.

NUMBERS AND DISPOSITIONS

We have no reliable figures for the forces engaged at Lewes. Contemporary estimates, tabulated below, fall into two categories: totals exaggerated beyond all reason, and more sober figures for the knightly contingents:

Source	Royalists	Rebels	Description
Rishanger (Chronicle)	300		Edward's retinue
Walsingham (Ypodigma)	400		Edward's retinue
Walter of Guisborough	70/700		Edward's retinue
Westminster Chronicle	400		Henry's retinue
Canterbury Chronicle	1,500	500	Knights
Gilson Fragment	3,000	500	Knights
Trinity manuscript	1,200	200	Knights
Rishanger (Two Battles)		15,000	Londoners
Rishanger (Two Battles)		50,000	Total
Waverley Annals	60,000	50,000	Totals
Winchester Annals	60,000	40,000	Totals
Worcester Annals	60,000	40,000	Totals
Peter of Langtoft		60,000	Londoners

The only comment required on the larger figures is that Domesday Book suggests London's total population, male and female, was 12,000, a figure which might have doubled by 1264.

It is probable more foot were present than mounted men, but since the proportion between the arms is unknown, knightly numbers are no guide to total strengths. The skeletons buried near the prison, plus 500 more found at the priory, suggest fatalities exceeded 2,000. The finds are presumably incomplete, however, and we do not know what percentage of combatants was killed. Army size matters. It determines frontages occupied, time required to deploy and the duration of combat. Given armies of similar capabilities, it is a major determinant of victory. Victorian historians, who accepted fanciful contemporary statements, were puzzled by the lack of physical evidence for a struggle involving over 100,000 combatants, more than can be documented for any battle in the British Isles. The rapid collapse of one rebel wing suggests the numbers engaged were nothing like so large.

Plausible estimates of royalist mounted numbers are the Canterbury Chronicle's 'nearly fifteen hundred knights, well horsed and equipped with arms', and the Trinity manuscript's 1,200. Several sources give partial numbers compatible with these totals if multiplied up – for example: the 400 armed men of the king's bodyguard (Westminster), or the Lord Edward's retinue: 400 according to Walsingham, 700 according to Guisborough. The latter actually says 70, but the Latin words for 70 and 700 are nearly identical, suggesting a copyist's error. The Worcester Annals describe Edward's retinue as 15 banners, which at 10–20 men apiece supports the lower number. Contemporaries agree the dead were commoners, so the 2,000 skeletons were presumably royalist foot. Rebel fugitives must lie north of the battlefield, where a few have turned up. If half the royalist foot were slain and found, the king's army approached 5,500 men: 1,200–1,500 mounted, the rest on foot.

Modern accounts accept contemporary claims that the rebels were heavily outnumbered: the Dunstable Annals say by 4-to-1; Canterbury says 3-to-1 in knights; the Trinity manuscript and Gilson 6-to-1. All four are pro-Montfortian; they probably exaggerate. A miraculous victory against the odds would provide more convincing proof of the righteousness of their cause. Wykes, a royalist partisan, supports rebel claims, but his testimony is ambiguous: he also refers to multitudes of rebels; he criticizes Henry's decision to fight; and he had his own agenda. Wykes regarded the royalist sack of Northampton as a war crime. The royal host were sinners; the greater their number, the more salutary their punishment. French accounts of Agincourt stressed their own side's numerical superiority for similar

The Norman arch through which Edward's men marched out of Lewes Castle. Even the small numbers described in the text would need a couple of hours to defile through the narrow gateway. (Postcard from author's collection)

moralistic reasons. Sceptics who feel religious fervour, and an 8 per cent gradient might not outweigh odds of 3-to-1 may, view rebel numbers as understated. Controlling London's demographic resources, brought up by easy stages along a good road, Simon may have equalled or outnumbered the king in infantry.

Dispositions are better documented. Several contemporaries describe the royalists in three bodies, the rebels in four. Rishanger's Chronicle is typical:

> Edward, the King's eldest son, commanded the first battle, with William de Valence, Earl of Pembroke, and John de Warenne, Earl of Surrey and Sussex. The second, the king of Germany [Richard of Cornwall] with his son Henry; the third King Henry himself. The barons' army was divided into four battles. The first of which Henry de Montfort and the Earl of Hereford [actually his son] commanded; the second Gilbert de Clare, with John fitzJohn and William of Munchensy; the third, in which were the Londoners, Nicholas of Seagrave; the fourth Earl Simon led himself, with Thomas of Pelvestone.

Guisborough adds that Guy de Montfort accompanied the rebels' first battle, demonstrating the presence of reinforcements from the Midlands. Wykes describes

Edward's division as the flower of the army. Including Lusignans and Marchers, it was a glittering retinue for the royal family's rising star. If his wing was really 700 strong, Edward had half the royalist cavalry. The three leading divisions of each army are enumerated right to left, placing Edward opposite the Londoners. Leaving the castle via the gatehouse into Western Road, he would naturally find himself on the right, relegating his father and uncle from the priory to the less honourable left and centre. Suggestions that Simon cynically placed the Londoners in Edward's path appear far-fetched.

Modern accounts agree that Simon held his fourth division behind the others as a reserve. His co-commander's London connections suggest this division also included troops from the capital. The royal army had no reserve, having left 20 banners at Tonbridge. Assuming ten to 20 men-at-arms each, these might have mustered 300 riders, perhaps explaining the difference between the Canterbury and Trinity figures. Some modern accounts claim reserves were unusual in medieval battles. This is quite untrue. William Marshal had used reserves to win his tournaments; at Lincoln he effectively held three-quarters of his army in reserve, forming his four divisions in column.

Some accounts describe the royalists as surprised, hurried into action piecemeal. Wykes says Henry had believed the rebels unlikely to venture anything against him. Guisborough says 'the king had not considered the barons' approach so imminent', but the context suggests any surprise was more strategic than tactical. Royalist foragers, gathering hay on the Downs, roused their masters in time not just to arm themselves, but to foregather in the priory and seal a document. Rishanger suggests a prompt rather than disorderly response: 'The king, indeed, and his army … having realised [the rebels'] sudden appearance, awoke the more swiftly to put on their arms, and having drawn up their battle lines for fighting, spread their banners, one with a royal device threatening death, which was called the 'Dragon', [and] advanced with a monstrous great noise of trumpets'. A Montfortian source suggests the rebels deliberately refused to take the enemy in their beds: 'For they said, "We will await them here, and take advantage of their having some distance to climb; for if we were to attack them sleeping, we should be putting ourselves in the wrong".' (Waverley).

The downland track along which Simon de Montfort advanced, looking south towards the sea: the path curves leftwards, following the spur towards the prison. The undergrowth is modern: medieval sheep would have kept the ground clear. (Author's photograph)

The previous day's defiance guaranteed the enemy would fight; by closing up to the town Simon made sure they had no room for anything else. His own line faced east, extending roughly north–south across the spur marked by the 200ft contour, his centre near the track that runs past the prison to become Spital Lane. Assuming minimal gaps, the infantry of his three leading divisions might occupy just 500 yards from the main Brighton road on the right, nearly to Nevill Crescent on the left. This is a narrower frontage than usually allowed. It is calculated as follows:

4,000 foot	(allowing Simon numerical equality)
x ¾	(excluding the reserve)
x ¼	(assuming 4 ranks)
x 2/3	(allowing 2ft per man, the least practical frontage) = 500 yards

A narrow frontage has the advantage of keeping the Londoners clear of the steep ground between The Wallands and the Downs. Crossing this presents an unencumbered pedestrian with difficulties, let alone formed troops. Simon's reserve presumably lay behind his centre, a little higher up near the bend in the track.

The Royalist army needed more space, having all their troops in front, perhaps 600 yards. They presumably formed up several bowshot to the east, 400–600 yards away, where Western Road forks near the Old Windmill inn, now a private house. The divisions of each army marked their opposite number in the medieval fashion, advancing directly to their front. No contemporary specifies the distribution of mounted and dismounted troops. Most modern accounts assume the knights preceded their associated footmen. If this is correct, each division consisted of a few hundred knights and about 1,000 foot.

Simon, from his elevated position, could observe the fighting, and decide where best to intervene. The Royalist commanders could not. Their nominal chief, Henry III, was downhill on the left towards Winterbourne Hollow; the more dynamic Edward was equally downhill on the other flank towards Walland Park. Neither had an overall view of the battle, or any way of influencing its course beyond their immediate neighbourhood. Of the commanders present, only Simon could act as a general rather than as a local leader.

THE WRETCHED BATTLE OF LEWES

Thirteenth-century battles rarely lasted long. Small numbers and hand-to-hand combat quickly exhausted the participants. The Lewes Chronicle says the greatest part of the royal host was overthrown between *prime* and noon. Medieval timekeepers divided the day into 12 equal hours from dawn to dusk, their length varying with the season. In May an 'hour' lasted 77 minutes; morning started with sunrise at 4:15am, and ended as now at midday. Not all that time was spent fighting. The Worcester Annals say Henry III marched out during *prime*, sometime between dawn and 5:30am. The king's division would need almost two modern hours to defile in twos through Priory Gate, turn left along Southover High Street, march half a mile to the rendezvous, and form line.

CRY DRAGON! HENRY III AND HIS BATTLE STANDARD (LEWES) (PP. 50–51)

As the terrible clangour of the trumpets rings out, the dragon standard is unfurled (1), and the king's supporters (2) spur their destriers forward against the rebels on the hill above (3).

Heads, bodies, and limbs are fully encased in mail: only four knights died at Lewes. The richest, in front, wear fully enclosed iron helms, protecting the owner from anything but a lance point through the eye-slits. The gradient favours the rebels, but the royalists are more numerous. The day's outcome depends on the ability of the opposing horsemen to preserve their tight formation and achieve the greater impact.

A charge started at a walk, lances held upright, until the command 'Poignez!' – 'Spur on!' when speed increased to a trot. Couched beneath the right arm, each lance concentrated the energy of horse and rider in a single blow. Only at the last moment would the pace approach a gallop. As the lines crashed together, fragments of broken lances and shields flew about, the ensuing din of maces and swords upon helmets resembling a thousand blacksmiths beating their anvils.

A small group controlled the pace and direction of the charge. Its nominal chief was the lord king, Henry III (4), recognizable from his crown and the royal arms of England on his surcoat. Two of his most trusty knights hold his horse's reins, to frustrate hostile attempts on the royal person: Henry lost two horses killed that day. If the fight goes badly, his minders must extract their charge from the melee, and lead him to safety. In our reconstruction, this dangerous honour has fallen to Phillip Basset (5), who suffered 20 wounds at Lewes.

The attack's direction was indicated by the royal standard bearer (6). While the standard flew, nobody might seek safety in flight. Ours wears the arms of Hamo Lestrange, one of many royalist knights captured that day. Going into battle, Kings of England flew the dragon, a whip-like pennon formed like a snake, head towards the staff, tail writhing in the wind (1). Henry III's was 'of red silk, sparkling all over with gold, the tongue … made to resemble burning fire … continually moving, and the eyes of sapphires'. To signal the charge, musicians sound trumpets (7), playing as long as the banner remains standing. Beyond the king's closest companions ride lords and knights attendant upon the king, who will all be captured with him.

Edward would require just as long to arrive, suggesting hostilities could not have started much before 7:30am. This delay necessarily moves the battle nearer the town. It also bears out accounts that Richard of Cornwall's men were quartered in the town: if they too had needed to clear Priory Gate, the royalists could not have been ready before 9:30am, foreshortening events to an implausible degree. Starting in town, Richard's division would arrive first and occupy the centre, astride Western Road, covering the other divisions' deployment on either flank.

The battle consisted of three main events: (1) the Lord Edward's successful charge against the rebel left; (2) a rebel counter-attack along the rest of the line; (3) Edward's return. Many accounts imply Edward started the battle prematurely, before the other royalists were ready. The Chronicle of Battle Abbey, where Henry III stayed soon after the fight, contradicts these accounts, stating that he waited for Edward. The latter's alleged haste fits a lazy stereotype of youthful impetuosity. His apparent taking the lead probably reflects narrative convenience, authors working from one flank to the other. Wykes says everyone advanced together: 'the terrible war trumpets having sounded, the enemies fell upon one another *at once*, glaring grim faced' (author's emphasis). Guisborough and Rishanger confirm the simultaneity: 'prepared for deadly strife, a mass of infantry fell on as if *in a moment*', and 'thereupon unleashed, the squadrons *of both sides* swiftly threw themselves upon the enemy; and with cruel blows and a dreadful crash the sides came terribly together'.

De Montfort's left wheel around the curved track off the Downs may have brought his left flank nearer the enemy. Unless the Londoners knew how to mark time, which is unlikely with undrilled troops, they would forge ahead of their friends who were moving around the wheel's outer edge. The rebel front would thus cease to be straight, forming an echelon from the left. Guisborough applies a chivalric gloss to tactical happenstance, saying the Londoners particularly asked to strike the first blow. It was their bad luck to be opposite Lord Edward, who was 'thirsting like a stag for a spring of water for the blood of his enemies, the Londoners' (Rishanger). For once the personalized explanation may be true. Not long before, the citizens had pelted Edward's mother with stones and filth as she was rowed up the Thames.

Directing his followers against them, neglecting any attempt to co-operate with the other royalist divisions, Edward crashed into the rebel knights

French knights defeated and taken prisoner during the Second Crusade, painted by the francophobe Matthew Paris. At Lewes, English knights fled before Edward's Poitevin kinsmen. (MS 16 134v by kind permission of the Master and Fellows of Corpus Christi College Cambridge)

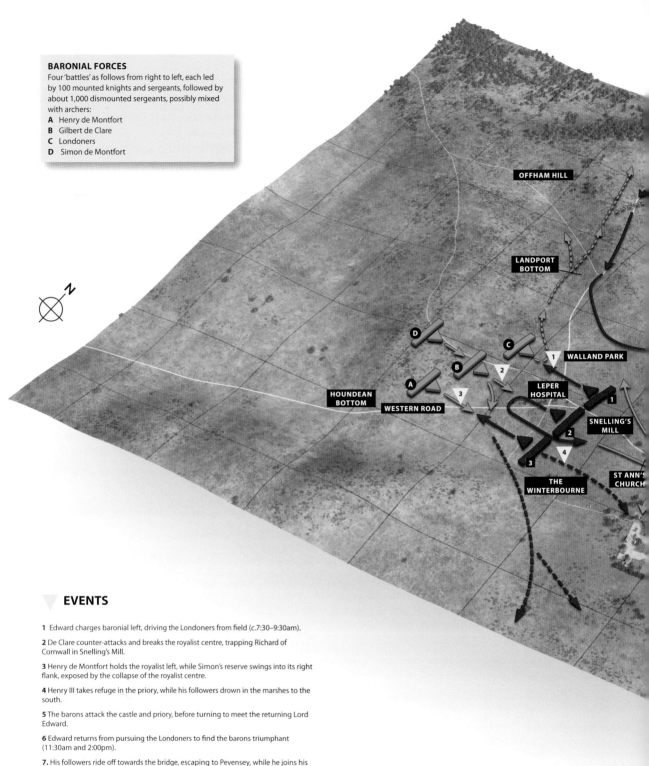

BARONIAL FORCES
Four 'battles' as follows from right to left, each led
by 100 mounted knights and sergeants, followed by
about 1,000 dismounted sergeants, possibly mixed
with archers:
A Henry de Montfort
B Gilbert de Clare
C Londoners
D Simon de Montfort

OFFHAM HILL

LANDPORT
BOTTOM

WALLAND PARK

HOUNDEAN
BOTTOM

WESTERN ROAD

LEPER
HOSPITAL

SNELLING'S
MILL

ST ANN'S
CHURCH

THE
WINTERBOURNE

▼ EVENTS

1 Edward charges baronial left, driving the Londoners from field (c.7:30–9:30am).

2 De Clare counter-attacks and breaks the royalist centre, trapping Richard of Cornwall in Snelling's Mill.

3 Henry de Montfort holds the royalist left, while Simon's reserve swings into its right flank, exposed by the collapse of the royalist centre.

4 Henry III takes refuge in the priory, while his followers drown in the marshes to the south.

5 The barons attack the castle and priory, before turning to meet the returning Lord Edward.

6 Edward returns from pursuing the Londoners to find the barons triumphant (11:30am and 2:00pm).

7. His followers ride off towards the bridge, escaping to Pevensey, while he joins his father (not shown).

THE WRETCHED BATTLE OF LEWES, 14 MAY 1264

The fighting at Lewes began with a royalist advance, the Lord Edward routing the baronial left, and pursuing it northwards off the battlefield. The rest of the baronial army counter-attacked, smashing the royalist centre, and holding the royalist left. Simon de Montfort's reserve then wheeled right, and drove into the king's flank. By the time Edward reappeared, the barons had won.

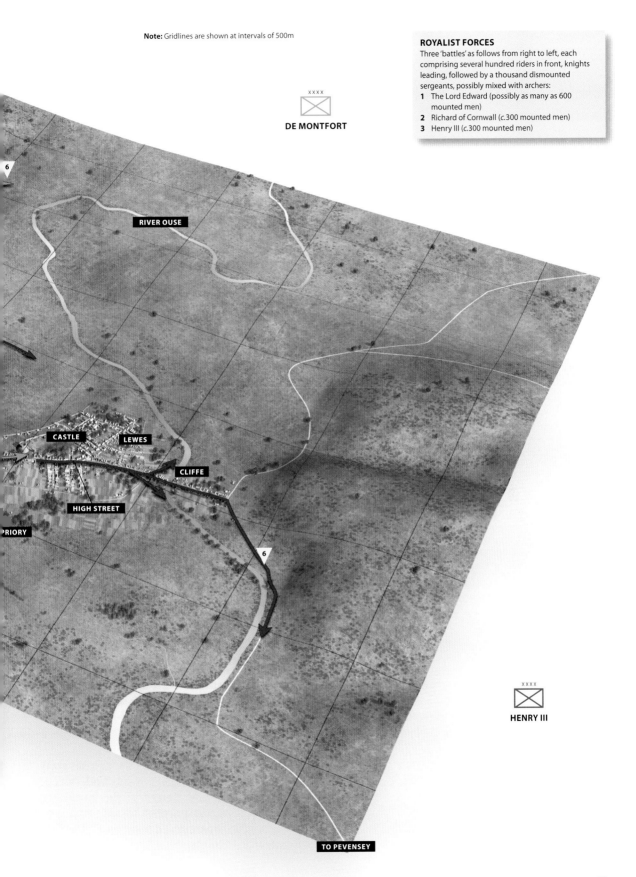

Note: Gridlines are shown at intervals of 500m

DE MONTFORT

ROYALIST FORCES
Three 'battles' as follows from right to left, each comprising several hundred riders in front, knights leading, followed by a thousand dismounted sergeants, possibly mixed with archers:
1 The Lord Edward (possibly as many as 600 mounted men)
2 Richard of Cornwall (c.300 mounted men)
3 Henry III (c.300 mounted men)

RIVER OUSE

CASTLE   LEWES

CLIFFE

HIGH STREET

PRIORY

6

HENRY III

TO PEVENSEY

before him, driving them back onto their main body. The baronial left was immediately shattered and broken through – *penetrata et dissoluta*. Seeing their standard-bearer fall, 'the immense crowd of Londoners inexperienced in war ... putting fear before courage, convinced itself that safety in flight was preferable to awaiting the chance outcome of battle' (Wykes). Their own chronicler admitted, 'at the first onset, the greater part of the Londoners, horse and foot, as well as certain knights and barons, took flight'.

Some went back uphill. Victorian quarrymen found their skeletons in Offham Chalk Pits. Others peeled off to the left along the banks of the Ouse, where 60 knights were reportedly drowned. Edward chased the fugitives 'for the space of four miles, dealing out the most dreadful slaughter; by whose absence the power of the king's army was much diminished' (Rishanger Chronicle). Edward's success was not surprising: the flower of the royal host attacking a multitude ignorant of the chances of war. Cynics might agree with Blaauw: heavily mailed knights on armoured steeds needed little courage to charge an inchoate mass of diversely equipped foot.

Meanwhile, the other baronial divisions smashed the royalist centre and left: 'The most part perished, and the King of Germany was taken, along with Robert Bruce and John Comyn, who had brought along numerous Scots. The king's battle was broken through, and his standard bearer killed' (Guisborough). Secondary accounts describe Richard of Cornwall's division staggering under a hail of stones and arrows from higher ground. The rebel breakthrough split the royal army in two. Richard's division was driven back into the town, a direction demonstrated by its leader's reappearance inside Snelling's Mill. The king's division retreated south across Winterbourne Hollow, past the priory, and into the tidal mudflats. The Lanercost Chronicle claimed an eyewitness saw scores of them at the ebb-tide, drowned in their saddles, their steeds mired in the slime.

The role of Simon's reserve is unclear. Thomas Wykes implies an enveloping movement: 'the kings of England and Germany ... left alone, surrounded by an infinite multitude, after a severe struggle, no longer able to resist the onset of the encircling masses, [fled] together to the priory' (*sic*).

Simon's charge downhill from the monument in the Priory: unseated on the right, Richard of Cornwall is identified by his coat of arms: *Argent a lion rampant gules crowned or, within a bordure sable, charged with bezants*. (Author's photograph)

This suggests Simon wheeled right into a royalist flank exposed by Edward's disappearance, or Richard of Cornwall's rout. There was much heavy fighting. Simon's own standard-bearer, a key target, was killed. Philip Basset, the royal justiciar, suffered 20 wounds before he would surrender. Even the enemy felt 'he deserved glory beyond the rest that day for giving and receiving blows' (Rishanger).

The rebels deliberately targeted the royalist leaders: 'The whole weight of the battle, the earl's purpose leading that way, was massed against the kings of England and Germany, chiefs of the whole multitude' (Wykes). Rishanger says, 'the Earl, a most sagacious warrior, and Gilbert de Clare and the other barons devoted all their efforts to the surrender of the king of England and the capture of the king of Germany, *so that the shepherd having been struck down, the sheep were scattered*'. Medieval battles, from Hastings to Lincoln, were usually decided by the fall of the defeated leaders. Much beaten with swords and maces, Henry had two horses killed beneath him before his bodyguards, seeing how the day had gone, led him back into the priory, 'shutting the gates, and setting guard with many knights' (Guisborough).

Henry's withdrawal and his infantry's slaughter were decisive. Scenting victory, 'the barons broke into the town, nor for a long time could the crowds of wounded be readily told apart, royalists from baronialists' (Guisborough). More rebels beset Richard of Cornwall in Snelling's Mill, accusing him of being a sorry miller, until he surrendered to one of Gloucester's knights. A contemporary rhyme features on a nearby plaque:

> Richard, though thou be a trichard [trickster]
> Trichen shalt thou never more.

Edward returned towards midday, or a little later. The Lewes Chronicle's closing the battle at noon may reflect Henry's retreat inside the priory. The Melrose Chronicle claims much of the day was spent fighting 'until the eighth hour'. That would end the battle about 2:30pm, not 8:00pm as sometimes said. Edward's charge and a 2- to 4-mile pursuit might take an hour, but gathering scattered riders would require longer. A. H. Burne, who fought in a war that featured cavalry charges, reckoned three hours for Edward to rally and return. Adding four hours to the different start times proposed here and in Burne's *More Battlefields of England* puts the prince's reappearance between 11:30am and 2:00pm.

Lewes Priory Gate and Southover parish church: monasteries were fortified physically as well as spiritually: the battle lost, Henry III's escort led him inside and placed guards around the priory walls. (Photograph courtesy of Jeff James)

THE SIEGE OF SNELLING'S MILL (LEWES) (PP. 58–59)

Swept away by the rout of the royalist centre, the king's brother, Richard Earl of Cornwall (1), takes refuge on the steps of Snelling's Mill (2), taunted by rebel foot soldiers (3) chanting a popular verse:

Richard, though thou be a trichard [trickster]
Trichen shalt thou never more.

A wealthy man, Richard's loans to the fiscally challenged Henry III had excited popular hostility. Reduced to walking by the death of his horse, he is heavily equipped in full knightly rig: including the great helm portrayed on his seal.

Richard's refuge is a post mill, named after the massive wooden pin on which the superstructure swivels on the trestle beneath to face the wind. Later the mill was misleadingly known as King Harry's, and confused with another built on the hill in the distance. Today, a plaque commemorates the mill's site in Western Road, a helpful pointer to the battle's location. In 1264, open downland extended along the road as far as Lewes town. Now built up, the open ground allowed the royalists to form up for battle near the leper hospital in the middle distance (4), facing the baronial forces on the slope beyond (5).

The lightly equipped baronial foot have overtaken Richard, blocking his retreat into Lewes. Some have mail *haubergeons*, a short version of the knightly hauberk, under their surcoats. Others wear a padded linen gambeson or *pourpoint*, a more comfortable alternative to mail. The baronial centre's leader was Gilbert de Clare, Earl of Gloucester, whose yellow livery they bear. On their backs, the rebels have sewn white crosses, the traditional badge of English crusaders, to demonstrate the righteousness of their cause. Self-equipped, the men carry an assortment of weapons, from swords and spears to long-handled axes.

Richard was too valuable a prize to be butchered like his men, whose mass graves were discovered beyond the hospital during construction of the prison (not shown). When the rabble have had their fun, he will be allowed to surrender to one of Gloucester's knights, Sir John de Beavs (6). In his turn, Sir John handed Richard over to his lord to be held hostage as a surety for the king's observing the peace terms agreed next day under the Mise of Lewes.

Edward might have returned sooner, except for an episode that features in every account of the battle, but had no bearing on its outcome. Earlier that year, Simon had injured his leg and had to travel by carriage. He had recovered enough by May to use the vehicle for transporting hostages held for the good behaviour of London's royalists. The coach and its occupants were left behind before the battle: on top of the Downs according to contemporaries; more likely on lower ground given the steep terrain. Flying Montfortian banners the carriage was irresistible bait for Edward's knights. Imagining Simon within, they slaughtered its luckless occupants. Some accounts allege a design to lure Edward's followers away. More likely the carriage was left with other transport, north of Offham, to be looted by the victorious royalists.

While Edward's men ransacked rebel wagons, the morning slipped away. When he returned, imagining a glorious victory, his troops were exhausted, their horses blown: 'nearing the place of the dead and viewing the extensive slaughter, their spirits sank and they lost their fierce looks' (Guisborough). Seeing their approach, the barons rode out to meet them. Most of Edward's supporters fled, led by his Poitevin kinsmen. Earl Warenne went with them, 'without a blow though not without blame'. Together they escaped to Pevensey Castle, whence they sailed for France. How they forced their way through streets clogged with both sides' dead and dying, is a mystery. Precipitated headlong down School Hill, fugitives piled up at the bridge, 'so that many fell off and were drowned'. The full moon being one day past, high

Cliffe Bridge in the 18th century: the Ouse is tidal and high water probably coincided with the royalist flight. Medieval bridges often lacked a parapet, and many fugitives were drowned. (Original watercolour courtesy of Eileen Brooks)

tide at Lewes on 14 May 1264 would occur shortly after 1:00pm, validating reports of mass drownings. Edward and the Marchers rode around the town to join the king in the priory, where the Waverley Annals unkindly says they exchanged their helmets for cowls.

Disorder continued: 'the townspeople … in an uproar on every side, for they were looting, pillaging, and catching the horses of the dead, and besides neither side could recognize the other' (Guisborough). The barons attacked the castle, whose defenders set the town alight with fire arrows. Next the rebels turned against the priory, which their own archers briefly set on fire. Excited by the castle's resistance, Edward proposed a sortie, but prudence prevailed. Next day, friars negotiated an agreement known as the Mise of Lewes. Edward and Henry of Almaine, Richard of Cornwall's son, were surrendered as sureties for the king's observance of the Provisions, the terms of which were to be subject to episcopal review. Government was placed in the hands of a council chosen by Simon de Montfort. The terms resembled those proposed before the battle, reflecting the unconvincing nature of his victory. The Canterbury Chronicle thought it should be 'attributed not to man's doing, but to the glory of God'. Casualties were heavy in proportion to the numbers engaged:

Source	Losses	Notes
Lewes Chronicle	600	Incomplete?
Mass graves	2,000	Found to date
Rishanger (Two Battles)	2,000	Plus 10,000 ran away
Trinity manuscript	2,070	
Worcester Chronicle	2,700	Buried: more drowned
Waverley Annals	3,000	Plus more drowned
Melsa Chronicle	3,300	
Canterbury Chronicle	3,567	Dover version
Furness Chronicle	4,514	
Winchester Annals	4,514	
Westminster Chronicle	5,000	
Rishanger (Chronicle)	5,000	
Rishanger (Two Battles)	5,000	Contradicts row 3 above
Wykes	5,000	
Osney	15,000	More than

We may assume similarities between literary sources represent plagiarism not corroboration. The archaeology supports the lower estimates. The Lewes Chronicle presumably included only those buried within the priory, to be found by Victorian railway engineers. Larger estimates may confuse casualties with total numbers engaged. The London Chronicle's 'countless multitudes slain' are nonsense, like the Osney scribe's 15,000. Enough Londoners escaped to clash with the Tonbridge garrison at Croydon on the way home. The Worcester and Trinity figures were probably identical before a copyist mistook *septingenti* (700) for *septuaginta* (70), or vice versa.

Only four persons of note were slain, two on either side, but the commons suffered heavily, especially King Henry's Scottish infantry, *jugulatis numero grande*. On the king's side 23 to 30 bannerets were captured. None escaped save the faithless Poitevins and their companions: 'On the barons' side nobody was captured, but many infantry killed' (Canterbury). Simon had enough of a victory to seize power and govern in the king's name, the first English magnate to do so. The question was whether he could make the 'Miracle of Lewes' stick.

THE CAMPAIGN OF EVESHAM

RENEWED HOSTILITIES

Simon struggled to convert his miraculous victory into political reality. The agreement to review the Provisions was dropped. Henry's closest kin remained in custody, the king himself reduced to a puppet. Overseas, the Pope threatened the new regime with spiritual sanctions, while the queen gathered ships and mercenaries in French ports. At home many royalists remained defiant, unwilling to recognize King Simon. Released to keep the Welsh in check, the Marchers broke out again in their usual fashion. Most dangerous of all, Gilbert de Clare turned against his fellow earl, motivated by Simon's alleged 'treachery', or plain self-interest. In January 1265, Simon called a parliament to legitimize his dictatorship. Banking on his popularity among the towns and lesser gentry, he summoned their representatives too, a first tentative move towards a House of Commons. They could not, however, replace the military muscle of the greater lords.

The break with Gloucester came at Easter in 1265. Simon had deployed troops to prevent a tournament that Gilbert de Clare and Henry de Montfort had planned for Shrove Tuesday at Dunstable. Like other rulers, Simon viewed tournaments as 'nurseries of discord'. When a rematch on 'Hockeday' (20 April) was cancelled, Gilbert withdrew to his West Country estates. Simon followed to the city of Gloucester, with the king and Lord Edward, but peace talks collapsed when a royalist force landed in Pembrokeshire. Led by William de Valence, the local earl, and John de Warenne, it included numerous paid knights and crossbowmen. Simon crossed the Severn and rode to Hereford, avoiding an ambush laid by de Clare. The move cut the invaders off from the great Mortimer castle at Wigmore, 19 miles (30km) north of Hereford. It also took Simon away from his own sources of strength, placing England's greatest river across his line of retreat.

Three weeks later, on 28 May, the royalist cause acquired fresh energy when Edward escaped while exercising on Widemarsh Common outside Hereford. The affair was carefully planned. Edward had been sent a particularly swift horse, which he did not mount until all the other horses present were tired out. He waited until a rider on a white horse appeared on nearby Burghill Nap, the agreed signal, and rode off at top speed, his unarmed guards turning back when they met Mortimer's rescue party. Next day, Edward met Gilbert de Clare, Roger Mortimer and John de Warenne at Ludlow, swearing on the host to observe 'the good old laws', abrogate 'the vicious customs that had arisen', deny foreigners valuable offices such as castle governorships and govern through a council of faithful natives (Wykes). De Clare had already mobilized his knights, sergeants and footmen. Reinforced by the Marchers and Warenne's mercenaries, they seized control of the Severn crossings, 'bridges were broken down, and boats sunk, and the fords dug out more deeply and watched, so that neither the king nor lord Simon de Montfort might get across the Severn. And on the other side of the sea, defences were constructed … so that they should not escape their enemies into Bristol' (Waverley).

Simon was isolated west of the river. He summoned a royal host to Worcester, but Edward took the city without a fight, and broke down the bridge. Simon changed the rendezvous to Gloucester, but that fell to the enemy on 14 June. A fortnight later the castle's garrison surrendered, saving their lives, arms and horses by swearing not to fight for 40 days. As at Northampton, Simon had lost a significant force before the war had started: Wykes states there were 'nearly 300 knights and other wellborn young men' present; Rishanger suggests rather fewer: five bannerets with their retinues. Before their oaths expired, the decisive battle would be fought and lost.

Meanwhile Simon sought an indirect way out of his strategic impasse. On 19 June, he made a politically costly agreement with Llywelyn ap Gruffudd at Pipton, signing away five royal castles in return for Welsh military assistance: 'And immediately, Llewellyn and his men on the one side, and lord Simon de Montfort on the other, doing much harm against the marcher lords and Gilbert de Clare, reduced their property in the Marches to nothing' (Waverley). Leaving chaos behind him, Simon marched deeper into Wales, taking hostile castles at Monmouth and Usk, menacing de Clare's Marshal inheritance in Gwent. By 4 July, Simon was at Newport, the king still in tow. Events suggest he hoped to take ship across the Bristol Channel, and join the Younger Simon then operating in Hampshire. The royalists reacted too quickly for him. Edward and de Clare took a shorter route, and cut Newport Bridge, trapping Simon the wrong side of the river Usk. Like the Marshal, de Clare kept a squadron of warships at his Chepstow headquarters, where the Wye joins the Bristol Channel. When Simon's shipping appeared, there ensued a rare naval battle in open water: 'the Earl of Gloucester despatched three pirate ships that he had, which are vulgarly called *galyas* (galleys) and at the same time he sent on board a large number of fighting men as well as mariners, who seeing the

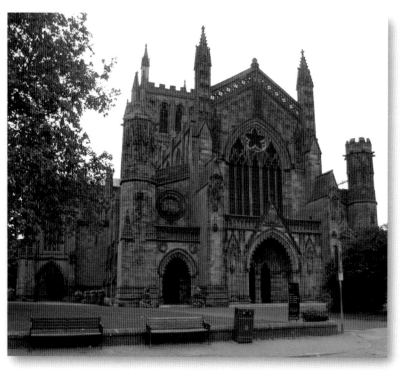

Hereford Cathedral, set deep in the Welsh Marches. Separating royalist groups at Wigmore and Pembroke, the city was a trap, the wrong side of the Severn and unable to nourish an army. (Author's photograph)

The South Wales Campaign, May–July 1265

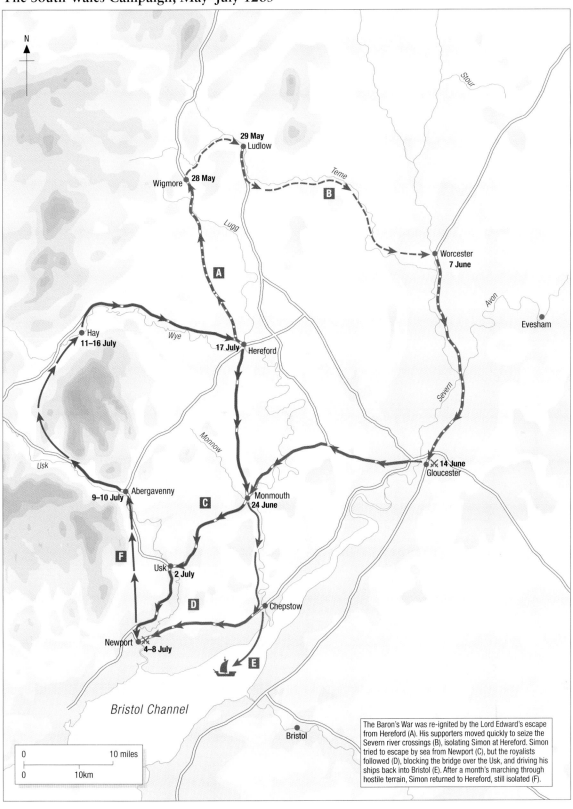

N

29 May
Ludlow

28 May
Wigmore

Teme

B

Stour

Worcester
7 June

A

Lugg

Evesham

Avon

Hay
11–16 July

Wye

17 July
Hereford

Severn

Monnow

✗✗ **14 June**
Gloucester

Usk

9–10 July
Abergavenny

C

Monmouth
24 June

F

Usk
2 July

D

Chepstow

Newport
4–8 July
✗✗

E

Bristol Channel

Bristol

0   10 miles
0   10km

The Baron's War was re-ignited by the Lord Edward's escape from Hereford (A). His supporters moved quickly to seize the Severn river crossings (B), isolating Simon at Hereford. Simon tried to escape by sea from Newport (C), but the royalists followed (D), blocking the bridge over the Usk, and driving his ships back into Bristol (E). After a month's marching through hostile terrain, Simon returned to Hereford, still isolated (F).

[Montfortian] fleet coming from Bristol, as it approached the shore, fiercely engaged them in combat on the high seas, of which they either took or sunk eleven ships, forcing the rest with bold attacks to put back' (Wykes).

Covered by bad weather, Simon burnt Newport Bridge on the night of 8/9 July, and silently withdrew to Abergavenny. From there he pressed on across the Black Mountains to Hay-on-Wye. His English troops, accustomed to eating bread, suffered horrible privations, since 'the only eatables in the land of Wales were meat or dairy produce, on which that people are accustomed to live' (ibid.). By 17 July Simon was back in Hereford. His situation was little improved, Gloucester having ordered 'the bridges all round to be broken, placing armed bands everywhere, who might deny men and supplies to the other side … so the Earl of Leicester and his troops might suffer a lack of food … and be destroyed' (ibid.).

THE YOUNGER SIMON'S CAMPAIGN

Pevensey Castle in East Sussex never surrendered after Lewes. The younger Simon was still trying to capture it when hostilities broke out again. Pevensey's massive Roman walls had been supplemented with a Norman keep and gatehouse. Then lying on the coast, it was easily nourished by sea, depriving Simon of the besieger's surest weapon, hunger. Wykes derided Simon's efforts as 'useless and worthless'; his more moderate Osney *alter ego* says, 'he spent much effort, but made little or no progress'.

The younger Simon's response to the emergency has been criticized as slow and faltering. This is an unfair view, inspired by knowledge of the outcome, which fails to acknowledge the difficulties of operating on external lines. The older Simon summoned help at the end of June, but royalist

Pevensey was a tough proposition for its Montfortian besiegers, the Roman defences reinforced by a Norman castle. Before the Haven silted up, seaborne supplies easily reached the garrison, making it impossible to starve them out. (Postcard from author's collection)

outposts on the Severn intercepted his messengers. Immediately certain news arrived, the younger Simon broke up his siege, and withdrew to London, where 'he summoned the barons, about 16 bannerets, and an infinite number of fighting men' (Wykes). Walter of Guisborough says nearly 20 bannerets and many commoners, suggesting metropolitan infantry. Simon's next move was into Hampshire, perhaps to rendezvous with his father in western England when the latter had passed the Bristol Channel.

Pleasantly overgrown today, Winchester's Roman walls were still a significant obstacle to an attacking army in the 13th century. Young Simon's men climbed in through a monastery window, and opened the gates from inside. (Author's photograph)

The day after St Swithin's Day (16 July) young Simon reached Winchester, England's second city and Henry III's birthplace. The inhabitants barred the gates against an army not led by the king: 'So, having introduced a band of armoured men through a window into the monastery of St Swithin's, which adjoined the city wall, and violently smashed the bolts and locks, pushing on in a terrifying manner, they gained entry' (Wykes). Once inside, the angry troops helped themselves to whatever they found in private houses or churches, targeting the Jews in particular, carting off 'an infinity of money'.

Simon presumably learned of his father's naval setback about this time, and turned north to Oxford: 'where, so their passage might be peaceful, the citizens of this crafty town did not deny them entry' (ibid.). Simon stayed three days, seeking news of his father who had just emerged from the Black Mountains. Moving on to Northampton, he and his associates developed a new strategy: 'that having distracted the Lord Edward and his companions, whom they believed beyond the Severn, they might proceed to Hereford to the assistance of the Earl of Leicester, so that increasing their army they might engage the enemy in battle, or bring him back with his men to the eastern parts [of the country]' (ibid.). After sunset on the last day of July Simon's army reached the defensive complex at Kenilworth, 'and having dined, and given tired horses their feed, with little forethought or precaution, fearing nobody, taking off the arms of war, because they thought themselves in safety, they slept on camp beds until morning' (ibid.).

The ruins of Kenilworth Castle from the causeway spanning its water defences. Marshy traces of the latter are still visible in the centre of the image. The large windows in the keep date from 16th-century habitability measures. (Author's photograph)

THE KENILWORTH RAID

The younger Simon's approach placed the royalists in an awkward position. Internal lines remain an asset as long as the enemy's forces are too far apart to combine and crush the central army between them. Edward had done his best to separate the two Simons, but now they were closing in, presenting him with an existential threat. Based at Worcester, Edward's forces were roughly equidistant between Montfortian hosts at Hereford and Kenilworth, 24 and 34 miles respectively (38km and 54km). For medieval armies this was striking distance.

Edward had to cripple one of the opposing armies before they could establish effective communications. He, or the Ludlow conspirators, chose to attack the younger Simon. He was more vulnerable, being less experienced and probably in less strength. The royalists were well informed of his movements by 'skilful scouts'. Guisborough describes a deeply imbedded espionage network, consisting of two operatives: Margoth, a female courier dressed as a man to allay suspicion, and Ralph of Ardern, a rebel co-conspirator, who deceived and betrayed them. Their intelligence revealed that young Simon's army lay in the open outside Kenilworth Castle, unlike the Earl's behind Hereford's city walls. Whichever rebel army Edward attacked, the Severn would protect his rear, as his men controlled all the crossings.

The timing of Edward's spoiling attack has caused confusion. Some modern accounts assume it took place the morning after Simon's arrival, while his men were still weary. Several contemporaries date the attack to the feast of St Peter in Chains, Saturday 1 August. Guisborough, however, specifies 'this was done the fourth *Nonae* of August', Sunday the 2nd. The London Chronicle agrees, saying Edward came the night *after* St Peter in Chains. Operational factors suggest the latter sources are correct. A messenger would take five hours to reach Worcester, trotting all the way. If Margoth set off at dusk (about 7:40pm) on the 31st she could not arrive before 1:00am the following morning. This is too late for a flying column to reach Kenilworth before dawn (about 4:30am). It seems more likely the royalists spent 1 August making ready, moving off that evening. Unqualified references to St Peter in Chains reflect the departure date, not the attack the next day.

Edward knew there were spies in his camp too. To confuse them, he avoided the direct route eastwards via Alcester. Wykes describes him leaving Worcester by the road north towards Bridgnorth and Shrewsbury, but assigns this detour to the night before Evesham. It makes better sense in the Kenilworth context, preserving surprise while heading in roughly the right direction. Two or three miles (3km and 5km) north of Worcester at Barbourne, the road forks east for

Kenilworth Castle before its slighting in the English Civil War. An engraving from the 1620s shows the extent of the bailey and the flooding that shielded its perimeter on both sides. (Postcard from author's collection)

The Younger Simon's Campaign and the Kenilworth Raid, July–August 1265

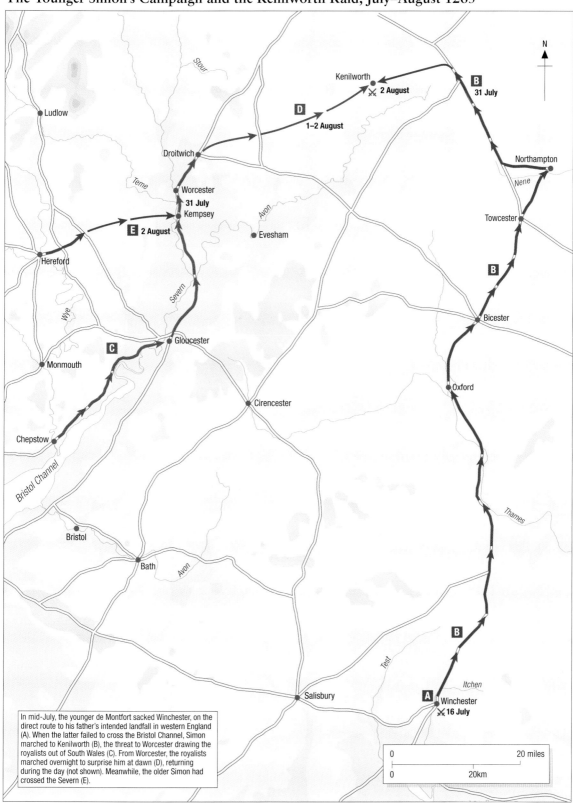

Ludlow

Stour

Kenilworth
✕ 2 August

D
1–2 August

B
31 July

N

Droitwich

Northampton

Teme

Worcester
31 July
Kempsey

Nene

Towcester

E 2 August

Avon

Evesham

B

Hereford

Severn

Wye

Gloucester

Bicester

C

Monmouth

Oxford

Cirencester

Thames

Chepstow

Bristol Channel

Bristol

Bath

Avon

B

Salisbury

Test

Itchen

A
Winchester
✕ 16 July

In mid-July, the younger de Montfort sacked Winchester, on the direct route to his father's intended landfall in western England (A). When the latter failed to cross the Bristol Channel, Simon marched to Kenilworth (B), the threat to Worcester drawing the royalists out of South Wales (C). From Worcester, the royalists marched overnight to surprise him at dawn (D), returning during the day (not shown). Meanwhile, the older Simon had crossed the Severn (E).

0		20 miles
0	20km	

Droitwich, towards Henley-in-Arden and Warwick. A mounted force starting at dusk, and marching more slowly than a messenger, might take seven hours to reach Kenilworth, arriving an hour before dawn without having slept. Wykes implies they even took some infantry in carts: 'dusk approaching, mounted in wagons, as if flying across the full width of the county, coming to Kenilworth as dawn arose, [Edward] took the whole lot sleeping in bed'.

Medieval Kenilworth consisted of two settlements, one along the present High Street, east of the castle towards the priory; the other south of the castle along the Warwick road. Complicating the tactical picture were extensive inundations created by damming the Finham brook. The distribution of these water features suggests Edward approached from the south, the shorter route and the least obstructed, to catch the rebels sleeping in the second more southerly settlement. Guisborough's repeated references to large numbers of common rebels, *multa plebe*, may mean their presence outside the castle was less through carelessness or exhaustion, than lack of space within.

Directed by Margoth, the royalists formed up in a valley near the castle, and put on their armour. Guisborough describes the valley as deep, but he lived a long way from the gently rolling Midlands. While the royalists were arming and adjusting their horses' girths, they heard wheels approaching. Fearing they had been betrayed, they mounted up and advanced lance in hand, only to meet some rebel supply wagons. Pressing on through the dawn, they fell on the sleeping camp, 'whom they awakened less gently than they expected' (Wykes). The pro-royalist London Chronicle says Edward ordered the enemy to be taken alive, but there was much slaughter of the commons. Simon escaped. Wykes and Rishanger say he was in the priory, and paddled across the fishpond in a small boat, others that he swam across naked. Boring Guisborough says Simon was already inside the castle. Ten, 13 or 15 knights banneret were captured and led back to Worcester in chains with their horses, banners and arms. Young Simon's army had suffered crippling losses in men and equipment. Depending on which number of prisoners is to be believed, between half and three quarters of his force was eliminated: ten to 15 banners out of 20. Edward and his allies returned to Worcester at once, demonstrating their grasp of internal lines.

The older Simon de Montfort was equally conscious of the fleeting opportunity that Edward's absence from Worcester represented. As the triumphant royalists returned from Kenilworth, the other rebel army was marching the other way: 'The Earl of Leicester, as his army was wasting away for want of food and drink, having abandoned Hereford by obscure country roads, lest he should be taken by the enemy, was intending with

The gatehouse at Kenilworth Priory where the Younger Simon may have spent the night before Edward's dawn raid. If the monastic perimeter was generally so well built, he might not have needed to escape across the mere. (Author's photograph)

premeditated cunning, by any means possible, to return to London' (Wykes). Other sources suggest a more positive aim: 'Unaware, therefore, of the terrible situation of his son, Simon Earl of Leicester left the Hereford area, and boldly crossed the Severn on the day after St Peter in Chains ... staying next day at Kempsey, he designed to catch the said Edward and Gilbert de Clare from one flank, while his son turned the other' (Waverley).

Kempsey was familiar territory. The manor belonged to Simon's ally the Bishop of Worcester. The Severn may have been lower lying then, possibly fordable. Gravel works hinder access to the east bank today, but a narrow sunken lane leads down to the far bank at Clivelode. The 13th-century authority Nicholas Trevet mentions a river crossing, 'next to a town called Clive'. This is usually associated with royalist operations at Cleeve Priory near Evesham. Dr D. C. Cox argues persuasively that Trevet meant Clivelode. The name is suggestive, combining Old English *clif*, a riverside slope, with *lad*, a ferry, one of which still operated there in the 20th century. Wykes actually says Simon crossed by boat. He then stopped at Kempsey for a day, awaiting news of his son, or for his army to finish crossing. Late on Monday 3 August, 'under night's silence', he marched for Evesham.

THE FIELD OF BATTLE

Evesham's topography is simpler than that at Lewes. Lying within a southward bend of the River Avon, the largest of several English rivers of that name, Evesham is protected on three sides by water. Its medieval bridge, repaired in 1256, led south-east towards Bengeworth, not south as the main bridge does today. A thousand yards wide at its closed end, the peninsula is twice that distance at its entrance, a broad front for a medieval army. Unlike Lewes, Evesham had neither walls nor castle, being a monastic dependency. The settlement lay north of the abbey, at the west end of the bridge. A port and market since the 1050s, Evesham was half the size of Lewes. A 12th-century rental lists 200 householders, suggesting the population numbered about 1,000. Gardens and orchards filled in around the buildings, with water-meadows along the river bank. Outside the enclosures lay arable land, covered with ripe corn, ready for harvest. Further north, Green Hill rises to just over 200ft (60m), an open area used as the town's common pasture.

The Victorian bridge that replaced the medieval structure across which Simon might have sought safety. The modern Avon is kept clear for river traffic, but the medieval river was no less serious an obstacle. (Author's photograph)

The junction at the top of Green Hill, the centre of the royalist deployment area. The left hand torn in front of the white house is the road from Mosham where Edward rested his men before the battle. (Author's photograph)

The main road to Alcester, 9 miles (14km) to the north, runs up the centre of the peninsula to crossroads at the top of the hill, around which the battle took place.

Numerous contemporaries describe Simon's army climbing the hill at the start of the action. Wykes may refer to its military crest, the line providing observation, mentioning a small hill which stopped Simon seeing the whole enemy strength until it was too late. Rishanger's Chronicle describes a broad field north of the town, suggesting an open area of common grazing land suitable for military evolutions. Within the crossroad's south-west quadrant lies an overgrown muddy patch known as Battle Well or Earl Simon's Well, which traditionally marks the place of his death. For tactical reasons, the royalist battle-line should lie a little further south, to give them the advantage of the slope, and deny the rebels access to the crossroads.

More substantial evidence links the battle with Offenham or Blayney's Lane, the crossroads' eastern arm. Eighteenth-century farmers reported 'innumerable bones' near its lower extremity in a meadow known as Deadman's Ait, with more in the arable land to the west. At the time, an ancient boundary stone called *Sifflaedestan* or Silvesdon marked a bend in the lane, near which the Evesham Chronicle placed the approaching troops. The 18th-century antiquary Ireland believed it had stood at the north-east corner of the field where the battle took place. A commemorative obelisk half a mile west of the crossroads, however, has nothing to do with the fighting. Erected in the 1840s by a local landowner as an ornamental feature, it has no historical significance.

Dominated by high ground to the north, with no artificial defences and an obstructed exit to the south, Evesham was a death trap. Earl Simon's presence there on 4 August 1265 must be seen as incidental, a point on a strategic trajectory unexpectedly intercepted by the enemy. Evesham lies almost halfway from Kempsey to Kenilworth, bypassing royalist Worcester by country roads to Pershore, then following the modern A44 south of the Avon. Green Hill and its crossroads might have been an ideal rendezvous for the two Simons: 14 miles (22km) from Kempsey; 24 miles (38km) from Kenilworth.

Once united, they could offer battle on even terms to the Marchers and Warenne's alien hirelings. Edward would then be the one cut off from the country's political and economic centre of gravity, as the de Montforts could block the main road from Worcester through Oxford to London. As at Lewes, the royalists would have had to fight facing their own lines of communication, doubling the stakes for them but not the rebels.

John of Oxnead's account of the campaign supports this analysis. Edward had intercepted Simon the Younger at Kenilworth, *revertentes ad Evesham*, heading back to Evesham. When the older Simon arrived there, he expected his son on the morrow, 'with a great army as he had commanded. For he did not know what had befallen him'. The Waverley Annals also say that, after the lord king's breakfast at Evesham, 'they all made their way towards Kenilworth, and the lord Simon de Montfort thought that his son Simon should be coming to meet them'. The younger Simon's reported presence at Alcester that day is consistent with such a narrative.

A. H. Burne has Earl Simon reach Evesham some time on 3 August, to spend the night there, without explaining why he did not press on immediately. Time was of the essence. Most contemporary sources say Simon left Kempsey at dusk on the 3rd, arriving at Evesham before dawn next day: 'Tuesday, the third day after St Peter in Chains' (4 August), (London Chronicle). Marching at 2½ miles an hour (4km/h) to spare his Welsh foot, a midnight departure would bring Simon to Evesham by dawn. His fatal error was stopping to refresh his tired troops, and hear Mass in one of the Abbey's side-chapels, now the parish churches of St Lawrence and All Saints. While Henry III took breakfast, Simon refused to eat. Perhaps he sensed imminent martyrdom; perhaps he was anxious to be gone. He was engaged in one of the most dangerous of military undertakings, a flank march across the front of an enemy army. Success demanded an inert opponent, an interposing obstacle or relentless speed. None of these conditions applied.

The churches of St Lawrence and All Saints (left to right): as laymen Henry and Simon would have heard Mass in one of these. The clouds recall unsettled conditions on the day of the battle. (Author's photograph)

THE ROYALIST APPROACH

The Lord Edward's night march from Worcester to Evesham has provoked wild speculation. The slenderest evidence has engendered the most remarkable strategic combinations. Recent evidence, however, casts fresh light on the royalists' approach. It provides an object lesson in the dangers of constructing complex narratives from a few words written far from the scene of action.

Traditional accounts of Evesham, often derived from the work of Sir Charles Oman or A.H. Burne, describe a complex triple envelopment intended to trap Simon in the bend of the river Avon by blocking the roads north to Kenilworth and the bridge behind him. Support for this narrative was found in contemporary statements describing Simon as hemmed in on all sides, the royalists approaching in three divisions. The latter have been treated as independent manoeuvre units, rather than tactical formations used in close physical contact with each other on the battlefield.

Walter of Guisborough's statements that Edward and Mortimer approached from the north and west have been lent the same broad operational sense. Simon's failure to escape across the bridge is presented as the tactical consequence of its being blocked, rather than a political act. The Waverley Annals make it clear that Simon deliberately chose 'a glorious martyrdom for the peace of the land ... although if he had wished he might very well have fled to Kenilworth'. Marching in widely separated columns would have been very dangerous for the royalists, exposing their detachments to piecemeal destruction. Such a plan implies they enjoyed a numerical superiority for which there is no evidential basis. The necessary detours would have involved Edward's men, still weary from their 70-mile round trip to Kenilworth, in hours of unnecessary marching, with all the uncertainties of keeping touch across a major river in the dark.

Fortunately the traditional schemes do not require detailed description. Publication in 2000 of a recently discovered account by a monk of Evesham Abbey has rendered nearly every previous reconstruction redundant. The exception was that of Dr Cox of the Vale of Evesham Historical Society. In 1988 he proposed that Edward simply marched his whole army straight to Evesham by the most direct route. Marching rapidly through Wyre Piddle along the Avon's north bank, the royalists intersected Simon's intended route at Green Hill, by the narrowest of margins.

The monk's testimony confirms Cox's interpretation. It names the riverside meadow at Mosham, between Craycombe Hill and Chadbury, where Edward and de Clare made knights together, while resting their horses and reconnoitring the ground. It describes Simon urging his younger followers,

The south-west quadrant of the crossroads where Mortimer's division formed up before the battle, having come over the hill to the left 'from the west and in the rear', as described by Walter of Guisborough. (Author's photograph)

men with families, to escape across the bridge. It places Mortimer, hitherto relegated to the cut-off party at the bridge, in the thick of the fighting. As battle commenced, it says the Bishop of Worcester withdrew to his manor at Blockley, across the still open bridge. The new source agrees with other neglected indicators. The London Chronicle says Edward and de Clare surprised Simon 'with all their army', not separate detachments. Five independent sources say Simon could have escaped, but would not: John of Oxnead, Rishanger, the Dunstable Annals and the Osney Chronicle, besides the Montfortian Waverley annalist.

Green Hill's eastern slope, looking south from de Clare's position behind the houses along the main road, showing how the ground falls away on either flank of the battlefield to the flood plain below. (Author's photograph)

There was no elaborate plan to surround Simon de Montfort. Edward relied on speed, concentration and luck. Wykes describes him as 'arriving at dawn, before sunrise, riding through the night'. He would do the same again before Falkirk in 1298. Reaching the decisive point at Green Hill before his opponent, he concealed two-thirds of his army to maintain surprise, and showed the rest to draw the rebels out. He then pursued his advantage to destroy the rebel leadership once and for all.

Evesham's bell tower, one of the few parts of the Abbey to escape destruction by Henry VIII. Built in the 1520s, it presumably replaced the earlier structure Simon's barber used as a lookout. (Author's photograph)

Alternative approaches to Evesham, 3–4 August 1265

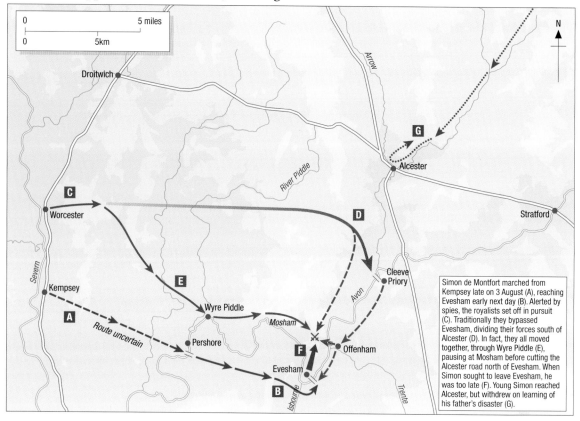

Simon de Montfort marched from Kempsey late on 3 August (A), reaching Evesham early next day (B). Alerted by spies, the royalists set off in pursuit (C). Traditionally they bypassed Evesham, dividing their forces south of Alcester (D). In fact, they all moved together, through Wyre Piddle (E), pausing at Mosham before cutting the Alcester road north of Evesham. When Simon sought to leave Evesham, he was too late (F). Young Simon reached Alcester, but withdrew on learning of his father's disaster (G).

This radical simplification of royalist movements allows us to reinterpret their deployment, not as three separate columns converging on the battlefield, but as the standard medieval array of three adjacent battles or *eschieles* moving up as a single operational entity. The Evesham monk says 'they came up the hill [from Mosham] in three divisions'; Guisborough is more expansive: '[Edward] having drawn up the line of battle in three *eschieles*, himself with his men on one flank, the Earl of Gloucester on the other, and Roger de Mortimer came in the rear'. Mortimer's rear division may have been smaller; Rishanger's Chronicle styles it a squadron or *turma*, rather than a battle or *acies*.

The simplest way for the royalists to form line was to move along the Fladbury road in column until de Clare's division had passed the crossroads, and then turn every man 90 degrees right, to create a line facing south. De Clare would be on the left, Edward in the centre and Mortimer on the right: 'coming in the west to the rear' (Guisborough).

Sent up the Abbey tower to spy out the approaching troops, Simon's barber surgeon reported, 'We are all dead men, for it is not your son coming as you thought, but the king's son from one side, the Earl of Gloucester from another, and Roger de Mortimer from a third' (ibid.). The monk's account confirms Gloucester was on the left, 'his banner coming up alongside over towards the river', which is nearer on that side.

Dr Cox converts this linear formation into an arrowhead, Edward leading, the wings refused in dead ground. This would allow Edward to see into the town, and use the forward slope to break the rebel charge, as Simon had done at Lewes: 'so that he might encourage the others to fight, he led the first battle himself … to undergo the first onslaught unflinchingly' (Wykes). To gain time, Edward employed a famous ruse: 'Lest they should be recognized at a distance, at first he flew the banner of Young Simon and the others who had been carried off prisoner, so he could gain possession of the steep slope of the hill, [against] the first shock of battle' (Guisborough). As at Lewes, the lie of the ground argues for moving the fighting nearer the town, away from the traditional battlefield.

The royalist arrival as one concentrated force removes the need for any great numerical superiority, although no contemporary risked an estimate. The royalists may have had a similar sized army to Lewes, de Clare's adhesion and Warenne's foreign mercenaries offsetting the absence of the previous year's feudal levy. The usable frontage across Green Hill is enough for 4,000–6,000 men in four to six ranks, if each front rank man occupied a yard. As winners, the royalists presumably outnumbered the rebels. The Dunstable annalist suggests, 'the lord Edward's party prevailed with an innumerable multitude'. The Osney scribe refers to Simon's 'somewhat scanty following': de Clare had defected; the Londoners were elsewhere. Claims that 200 rebel knights fell may be interpreted variously. If all the mounted rebels were slain, their original strength was half that mustered at Lewes.

EARL SIMON'S DEATH RIDE

The battle of Evesham was more political and religious theatre than military event: a prelude to the great Earl's martyrdom. Fighting was brief and straightforward. The interest lies more in de Montfort's reactions to the enemy's appearance than his tactics.

The Evesham monk saw what happened, and is our surest guide. Halfway through the morning, at *tierce* or the third hour (*c*.8:30am), Simon's scouts reported Edward and Gloucester 'coming from Worcester with their army … ready for battle'. The Osney chronicler says Simon was hearing Mass; Wykes that he and the king were mounted, ready to depart. More than one chronicler records Simon's agonized cry on the enemy's identification, 'God be prayed for our souls, then, since our bodies are theirs' (Guisborough). Some commentators doubt the captured banners anecdote, claiming Green Hill was too distant to distinguish heraldic devices, while the Evesham monk places the outburst later. If Edward's aim was to dash rebel hopes of reinforcement and encourage defections, he failed.

While his men ran to take arms, Simon bid farewell to his counsellor and friend the Bishop of Worcester, who retired over the bridge, weeping 'hot tears', urging the townspeople to seek refuge in the Abbey. Guisborough adds that Simon rebuked Henry de Montfort for the arrogance that had brought them to this pass, a tradition echoed in Peter de Langtoft's verse chronicle. The drama continued with a meteorological harbinger of earthly discord, as the sky darkened, and a torrential downpour swept across the battlefield. Observers in Oxford and London confirm thunder and lightning and heavy rain followed by calm. Rishanger recalled such darkness that monks could not recognize each other in choir, or read the scriptures.

While sheltering from the rain, Simon's followers discussed their options. One urged him to defend the monastic precincts. Men and horses were exhausted after three days without food or sleep, unfit for action until they had recovered. Simon refused, saying a knight's place was on the battlefield, the chaplain's in church. Like a Crusader, he was resolved upon defending his cause regardless of the outcome: 'And when it was urged upon him by his companions that he should fly to his castle at Kenilworth and so escape imminent death, that constant man steadfastly replied, 'it is not for the soldier of Christ to fly, but rather to fall by the sword of the enemy' (Osney). As the earl left the Abbey precincts, his standard-bearer broke his lance and banner against the archway, a sinister portent.

Nobody describes the rebel array. Events suggest the horsemen moved out first in a single body, followed by the foot. An oblong wedge of 200 horsemen eight ranks deep might occupy as small a frontage as 25 yards: narrow enough to advance rapidly; deep enough to punch a hole through the encircling host. The infantry fell behind at once, Simon rebuking its commander Humphrey de Bohun: 'that's no way to conduct a battle, putting the foot soldiers at the rear. I know well how this will turn out'. As the column passed the town conduit or *lavour*, the Earl urged his followers to save themselves and await better times. Sir Hugh Despenser, Simon's seneschal of the Tower, refused in biblical terms, 'My Lord, let it be. Today we shall all drink of one cup, just as we have in the past'. Passing the final houses, a quarter of a mile from the Abbey, the Welsh set up their traditional battle cry or *ululatio*, 'so that the whole earth seemed to echo against this frightful noise'.

The road runs level for the first 300 yards, then mounts a gentle gradient towards Green Hill. Not until the rebels reached its brow did they see the odds stacked against them, 'on the crest of the hill, not far from them, at a stone's throw' (Westminster). The Welsh fled immediately. Simon admired the enemy formation: 'and when he saw the enemy's line of battle, carefully and wisely deployed, he said to his men, "By the arms of St James" (for thus he was accustomed to swear) "they come on skilfully; but it is not by themselves, but from me that they have learned this. So let us commend our souls to God; for our bodies are theirs"' (Rishanger). Dr Cox suggests Simon meant the royalist use of high ground to slow an attack, as he himself had done at Lewes; Rishanger seems to refer more to their close formation, by which 'they had rendered their array impenetrable'. De Clare's banner drew a final bitter gybe, '"This red dog will eat us up today". For the Earl of Gloucester was red' (Furness).

At this tantalising point, the new manuscript breaks off, sending us back to traditional sources for the moment of impact. Dr Cox places this near the 150ft contour, where the main road follows a cutting through the brow of the hill, revealing a cross-section of the slope. A. H. Burne put the collision 600 yards further on, just before the crossroads, on more level ground. The first shock favoured the rebels: 'Lord

Simon's line of advance: the cutting reveals the cross-section of Green Hill's steep forward slope where Dr Cox locates Simon's climactic encounter with the Lord Edward. The car has just turned out of Croft Road. (Author's photograph)

Simon de Montfort and his son Henry and lord Hugh Despenser making a most vigorous charge against the enemy, broke into the opposing array by fighting, and laid many dead to right and left; and made a path back and forth through them. Wherever, indeed, Simon struck, he slew, or laid low, or dealt a deadly wound' (Oxnead). Robert of Gloucester says many of Simon's opponents fled, and had to be rallied. Eighteenth-century traditions of fighting in Offenham Lane, and the bones found nearby, suggest the rebels' impetus may have carried some of them that far.

THE MORDRE OF EVESHAM

Attacks on a narrow front naturally create a salient, with deep flanks exposed to counter-attack. This is especially so when, as at Evesham, the attackers lacked supporting echelons to distract the enemy on either side from wheeling inwards to crush the intruders between them. John of Oxnead evokes the moment the rebel attack ground to a stop, the enemy retiring before Simon's terrible blows, 'until the whole army made a circle around him, so the horse which he rode could not get through anywhere'. Momentum lost, there was nothing to stop de Clare's superior numbers enveloping Simon's right flank and lapping around his rear, sealing off the rebel spearhead while Edward held it in front:

> The Earl of Leicester, having at once seen [Edward's] leading battle … he pulled his army together, as it were into a circle, so they could sustain the enemy's threatening attacks more bravely… But the Lord Edward … attacking the concentrated mass in front … the Earl of Gloucester with a valiant band drawn from the second battle, falling promptly upon the opposing side all squeezed together in a heap, he surrounded the whole army as if joining the formation's flanks together (Wykes)

Brought to stand, the rebel knights became vulnerable to royalist footmen. Simon's horse was 'cut from under him by infantrymen', run through with swords and lances. Fighting on foot, Henry de Montfort was 'cleft in two with a sword' before his father's very eyes. Hugh Despenser, 'fatally denied safety, fell stabbed with a dagger' (Wykes). Even the king was a target, borne along in Simon's train in a borrowed hauberk, shouting, 'I am Henry of Winchester, your king, do not kill me'. Wounded in the shoulder by a Marcher's javelin, he was recognized by chance, and escorted to safety by Edward's knights. The royal accounts confirm Henry's plight, writing of two silver-mounted belts he lost during the battle.

A Victorian view of Simon's last stand, beset with infantry in unlikely headgear. The recently discovered source, portrays him as victim of a mounted attack by picked men-at-arms. (Author's collection)

'WHAT MERCY FOR TRAITORS?' – THE DEATH OF SIMON DE MONTFORT (EVESHAM) (PP. 80–81)

Early on Tuesday 4 August 1265, a chosen band of killers strike down the great earl **(1)**, decapitating the baronial cause.

The deaths of Simon de Montfort and his closest companions at Evesham brought baronial resistance to Henry III's arbitrary exercise of royal power to a sudden and brutal end. The deliberate killing of such high-status individuals was deeply shocking. Usually knights were granted quarter, and held for ransom. The splits in England's ruling elite, however, ran too deep. Simon's opponents swore he must die. Approaching the battlefield, they nominated 12 knights led by Roger de Mortimer **(2)** to do the deed.

Disregarding the encircling carnage, they forced their way through the press to reach the earl, where their leader 'struck him through the neck with his lance, and it was Sir Roger de Mortimer, for he could be recognised by his armour'. Hugh Despenser, the Tower of London's baronial seneschal, was cut down at Simon's side **(3)**. At least 34 other rebel knights perished in the massacre.

Green Hill was open common land. It had no obvious feature to pinpoint the tragedy's location, whether at the crest, near Battle Well as generally believed, or nearer the town at 'Godes Croft'. Today's remaining farm land is arable; in 1265 it was pasture, the grass trampled by hundreds of hooves, throwing up a cloud of dust to hide the shameful blow.

Simon's coat of arms comes from a carving in Westminster Abbey. An earl well tried in war, he would have the latest protection, such as the flat-topped helm. Improved body armour of iron plates or boiled leather are probably concealed beneath his surcoat.

Mortimer's appearance is undocumented. A major landowner, he could afford the costly items shown here: full facial helmet and horse armour. Made in two sections to cover front and rear parts of the animal, the latter is usually hidden beneath cloth trappings. The other assassins are unidentified. Here they take a supporting role, except the knight lunging forward to hack though Despenser's hauberk **(4)**. Their lesser status is reflected in their simpler mail coifs **(5)**. Both sides at Evesham wore crosses to distinguish themselves from the enemy: white crosses for the rebels, red for the royalists.

Simon held out, 'bravely fighting against the infantry, defending himself until his enemies dismounted from their horses, basely took him from behind, stripped off his armour, and thus naked killed him. Who, however brutally and dishonourably treated, never spoke any word, much as they might say, "Traitor, surrender". He made no reply, but steadfastly with his last breath said, "Dieu, merci", and so gave up his life.' (Oxnead). Guisborough says Simon did seek quarter, but was denied: 'What mercy for a traitor?' they replied; the Osney Chronicle has his enemies shouting, '"Old traitor, old traitor, it is impossible that you should live any longer".'

Several sources assert Simon was killed in Edward's absence and against his will. Wykes blames 'the base crowd of foot, who especially hated his doings', a statement at odds with every indicator of contemporary opinion. We now know, thanks to the Evesham monk, that the royalists at Mosham, 'designated twelve of their strongest and most intrepid men-at-arms … to kill the Earl of Leicester, and break through the ranks forcibly and rapidly … until they reached the person of the earl'. The new account resumes just as the assassin 'struck him through the neck with his lance, and it was Sir Roger de Mortimer, for he could be recognized by his armour'. A few daring sources hint at the death plot: Rishanger refers to 'premeditated conspiracy'; Langtoft says Edward and Gilbert swore 'they would take Earl Simon and his sons, and without accepting ransom put them to death', a pledge confirmed by Wykes' colleague at Osney.

Simon died 'not so much defeated as overwhelmed … delivered mercilessly unto death' (Rishanger). Others saw his defeat as the product of hard fighting and the adverse fortunes of war. Langtoft sang, 'Hard was the battle and great the folly'. Wykes' language echoes secular knightly literature: 'either side struggling horribly, the surrounded host could not resist the encircling attack, while shields having been split through in vain, the web of mail shirts hacked into pieces, lances broken, swords gorged with blood, they gave ground without resistance. So it was that they who emerged triumphant from the battle of Lewes, having suffered the fickle turn of fortune … nearly all run through with swords, wretchedly met their end.'

This final paroxysm of violence is usually located near Simon's Well, 145 yards south-west of the Green Hill crossroads. Hallowed by miracles and centuries of tradition, the site of Simon's death appears firmly established, conveniently opposite Mortimer's position on the royalist right. In August, however, the well is a waterless depression in the ground. It was 'discovered' the year after the battle, by outsiders unaware of the spring's intermittence, and probably devoid of local knowledge. Modern students of the battle should beware. Wells were often associated with figures of popular veneration, perhaps an echo of pre-Christian beliefs. Battle Well's physical location 120 yards west of the rebel axis of advance is tactically unsatisfactory. Dr Cox placed Simon's death nearer the rebel line of attack, following the Lanercost Chronicle which says he died at 'Godescroft'. Cox identified God's Croft with a 19th-century house near the junction of the main road and Croft Road, 300 yards below the crest of Green Hill. The location is persuasive, if

The traditional site of Simon's death at Battle Well south-west of the top of Green Hill. Almost dry in summer, as here, it was 'discovered' two years after the battle by passing strangers. (Author's photograph)

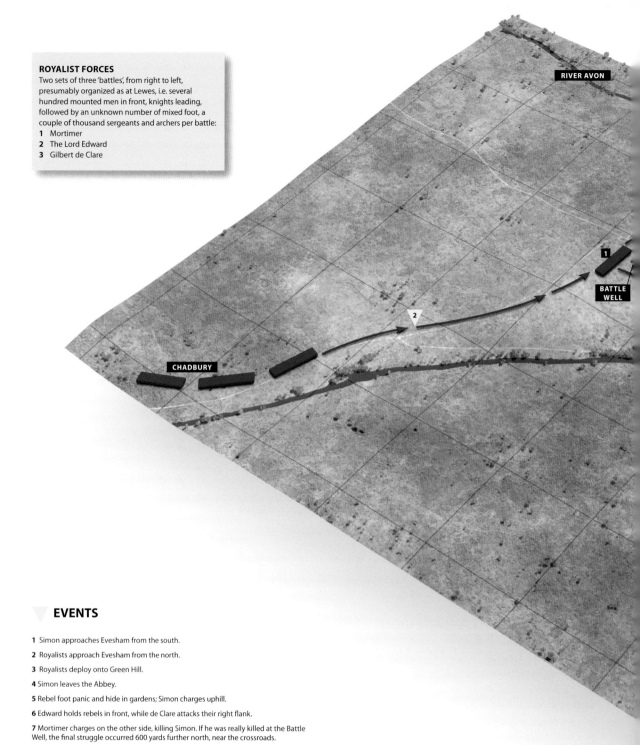

RIVER AVON

1

BATTLE WELL

2

CHADBURY

▼ **EVENTS**

1 Simon approaches Evesham from the south.

2 Royalists approach Evesham from the north.

3 Royalists deploy onto Green Hill.

4 Simon leaves the Abbey.

5 Rebel foot panic and hide in gardens; Simon charges uphill.

6 Edward holds rebels in front, while de Clare attacks their right flank.

7 Mortimer charges on the other side, killing Simon. If he was really killed at the Battle
Well, the final struggle occurred 600 yards further north, near the crossroads.

THE MURDER OF EVESHAM, 4 AUGUST 1264

Simon de Montfort reached Evesham about dawn, and stopped to refresh his troops (1). Soon afterwards,
his royalist pursuers appear from Worcester, heading for Green Hill, north of Evesham (2), where Edward
occupies the forward crest (3). Scorning flight, Simon leaves the Abbey to meet him (4). Simon's infantry
panic on seeing the enemy, but he charges up the hill (5). While Edward absorbs the impact, de Clare attacks
Simon's right flank, forcing the rebel knights into a ring, and driving them downhill (6). Mortimer then
charges through the melee, killing Simon near 'Godescroft' (7).

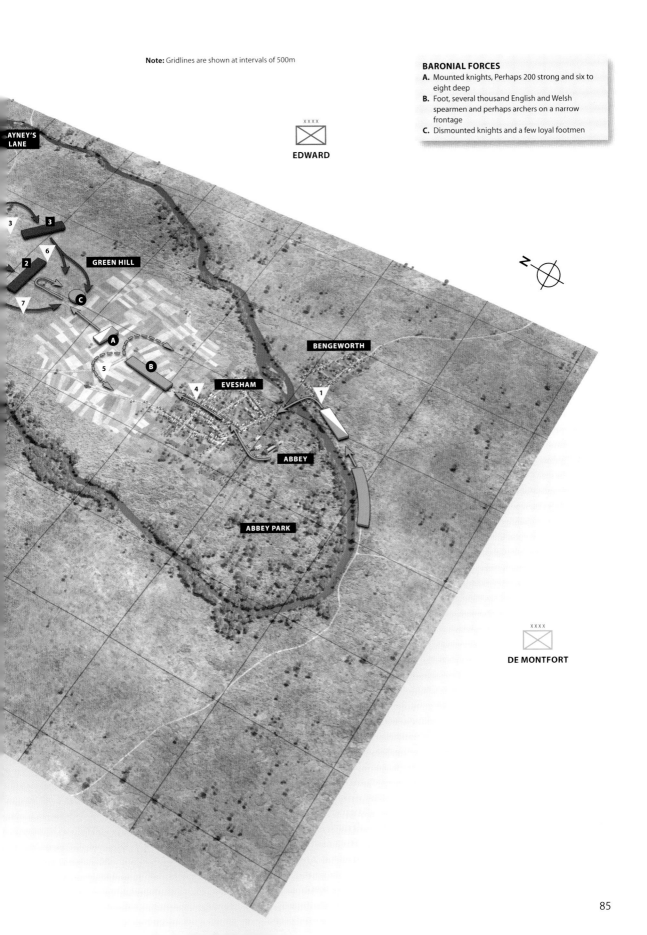

Note: Gridlines are shown at intervals of 500m

AYNEY'S LANE

GREEN HILL

BENGEWORTH

EVESHAM

ABBEY

ABBEY PARK

EDWARD

DE MONTFORT

BARONIAL FORCES
A. Mounted knights, Perhaps 200 strong and six to eight deep
B. Foot, several thousand English and Welsh spearmen and perhaps archers on a narrow frontage
C. Dismounted knights and a few loyal footmen

one imagines the rebels were stopped before reaching the hill's highest point, and pushed back down the slope by superior numbers, rallying in some enclosure or 'croft', where they became trapped.

Almost everyone agrees the battle was over quickly, as might be expected of an unsupported cavalry charge against the odds. The Westminster Chronicle says Simon fell in the first clash, *primo conflictu*, and all those with him killed or captured in a very short space of time. Rishanger says it was all over between *prime* and *tierce*, two and a half hours, including arming, discussing and forming up. The younger Simon had marched up from Kenilworth, but had no time to intervene. Robert of Gloucester lamented his stopping to eat at Alcester. Fugitives told him of his father's disaster, implying some had broken clean through the enemy line to safety. Wykes gives more detail, possibly from Richard of Cornwall, held hostage at Kenilworth: 'His son Simon looking on, bringing fresh help to the finished battle, and having seen from a distance, returned to Kenilworth's fortifications ... And there with gloomy spirits, he lamented the death of his father and brother, and it is believed took neither food nor drink for many days.'

Sources like Guisborough who say fighting continued until evening may mean the ensuing massacre. Royalist losses were negligible, at least among the gentry. Two or three knights or squires were killed having failed to wear the red crosses their friends used to distinguish themselves from the rebels' white. Few rebels can have escaped the fatal bend in the river. The Evesham monk lamented, 'God alone knows how many of them there were'. Rishanger's Chronicle listed 12 named knights banneret all killed, besides 'others of lesser degree, a great multitude of sergeants and infantry, and an excessively great number of Welsh'. These had fled first, 'hiding in cornfields and gardens, and fleeing all over the countryside, [they were] subsequently discovered and killed'. Our monk describes corpses, 'thick and dense upon the ground like animals', littering fields and streets. Even the sacred Abbey was defiled with blood running down the altar into the crypt.

Croft House, which Dr Cox identified with the recorded site of Simon's death at 'Godescroft'. Near the main road in Croft Road, on Green Hill's forward slope, this location is tactically more convincing. (Author's photograph)

Most shocking to contemporary opinion was the deliberate elimination of rebel leaders. The disorders of Stephen's and John's reigns had never seen such wholesale slaughter of gentry as was reported at Evesham: 'For on the Earl's side there was not any man of courage, valour, or fortitude who escaped death, except only Sir John FitzJohn ... taken under the protection of Sir Roger Clifford' (Osney). Wykes claimed 160 knights were killed, 'and an infinite number of nobles not yet knighted'. Robert of Gloucester remarked, 'such was the murder of Evesham for battle it was none'. Historians struggle to verify the chroniclers' claims, which sometimes count prisoners as dead. Dr Cox lists 39 individuals reported slain, including three royalists. He also names 16 prisoners, to whom can be added Humphrey de Bohun, who died of wounds. Over-reporting of rebel casualties was to the government's advantage, impressing public opinion and intimidating opponents. Two centuries later, Yorkist propagandists exaggerated Lancastrian losses after the battle of Towton for similar reasons.

Riddled with wounds, Simon's body became part of this propaganda war. Hands, feet, and head were all cut off, leaving a limbless trunk, 'lich a stok', in John Capgrave's Middle English. Impaled on a spear, the Earl's head, genitals stuffed in its mouth, was sent to Lady Mortimer at Wigmore. Such treatment was deeply offensive. Rishanger denounced it as 'contrary to the usage of the knightly order', comparing Simon to John the Baptist, his salted head served up at a feast. Knights in difficulties were usually spared, but things had gone too far. Edward and the king had been humiliated by defeat and captivity; Mortimer's lands devastated; Gloucester's honour tarnished by his own inconstancy. Simon's death satisfied an emotional craving for revenge, as well as removing their chief political enemy: 'After the battle was thus given, certain friends of the dead earl weeping and grieving ... came into the field and put his remains, which had been left in the open air, onto a dilapidated ladder, and covered the horribly mutilated remains and carried them to Evesham Abbey, and wrapping them in linen cloth buried them in a new tomb' (Osney).

Sources mindful of royal favour say this was done with Edward's approval. The Evesham chronicler was more realistic, saying the monks buried the rebel leaders 'in less than honourable fashion out of fear'.

Dedicated to Simon's memory by the Speaker of the House of Commons in 1965, this plinth marks the approximate site of the Abbey's High Altar. Seven hundred years earlier it witnessed the battle's final frenzy of slaughter. (Author's photograph)

AFTER THE BATTLE

Kenilworth's shattered keep, showing the massive walls that withstood King Henry's trebuchet stones. It took gunpowder to demolish the north wall when the castle was slighted in the 1640s. (Author's photograph)

Restored to royal power, Henry III was no more capable of ending the war than of preventing or winning it. His vindictive incompetence ensured two more years' fighting, despite the baronial cause's decapitation. The younger Simon held out in the Isle of Axholme in Lincolnshire, surrendering to Edward on terms that the latter broke. Fearing imprisonment in the Tower, Simon fled overseas. His mother, no longer recognized as the king's sister, had gone already. Guy followed once he had recovered from the wounds he suffered at Evesham.

A month after Evesham, a victor's parliament was held at Winchester to disinherit the king's opponents. William Marshal had been wiser in 1217, returning estates to their pre-war owners, but Henry despised his moderation. Instead, Henry created the conditions for further conflict. Not until May 1266 did Henry of Almaine disperse the northern disinherited at Chesterfield, while Edward chased 'brigands' along Hampshire's secret by-ways. The survivors of Chesterfield fled into local forests pursued by the Sheriff of Nottingham's archers, a curious inversion of the Robin Hood legend which may date from this period.

The Midland disinherited required more sustained efforts. Some 1,700 'valiant men' occupied Kenilworth after Evesham, raiding the countryside and ambushing the king's younger son Edmund. Almost a year after Evesham, about the feast of St John the Baptist, 24 or 25 June, a royal host invested Kenilworth on four sides. Worsted in *bikering* [sic] with the garrison, and fearing to assault the Earl's new fortifications and 'unheard of engines', the royalists settled in for the long haul: 'having set up nine machines all around, which were called *Blidis* [sic], they did not stop throwing stones, smashing the others' wooden buildings and towers, and hoping to knock down the masonry, [but] could not damage it at all' (Dunstable). The garrison held out until December, hoping for relief from Simon the Younger. Enfeebled by shortages of food and drink, stricken with dysentery, facing a winter without firewood or shelter, they surrendered on the 20th, 'having saved life and limb, horses and arms'. Wykes retails what must be eyewitness testimony to the garrison's pale faces and grey skin, the suffocating stench that greeted the besiegers on entering the shattered fortress.

Popular support for the baronial cause expressed itself at Evesham with a cult of the martyrized Earl. Some 130 miracles were reported in 1265–66, pilgrims coming from as far away as East Anglia and Kent. The government reacted vigorously, placing armed guards on roads into Evesham, replacing the abbot, and forbidding reference to the excommunicated Simon's supposed sainthood, or his 'vain and foolish miracles'. Fearful of showing Simon's tomb, the monks moved his remains to an obscure and unconsecrated corner of the abbey. Government repression was effective, although Edward II would be entertained with tales of Simon de Montfort in the next century. Miracles dwindled in line with fading political tensions. The drawn-out siege of Kenilworth provided an opportunity for the papal legate, Ottobuono, to persuade Henry III to allow penitent rebels to redeem their estates. The following June, the weathercock Earl of Gloucester occupied London, compelling the king to soften his terms, finally ending hostilities.

Simon de Montfort's defeat at Evesham was a key step in the development of strong English government, limited by representative institutions. While his death prevented England fragmenting into a patchwork of independent lordships like Germany, the parliament he summoned set a pattern for future

A Victorian impression of the trial of Edward II's favourite Piers Gaveston by angry barons in 1312: English politics became more cruel after Evesham. Edward and Piers were both killed. (Postcard from author's collection)

assemblies. Taxes raised for Edward's crusade in the late 1260s were negotiated with representatives of the towns, as well as the upper classes. If Henry III rejected the personal constraints of the Provisions of Oxford, he accepted the baron's local government reforms. The savage repression of the baronial attempt to subject the monarch to constitutional control, however, ensured that future failed kings, from Edward II to Charles I, suffered more drastic treatment than Henry III, earning the English a sinister reputation as regicides.

Old hatreds flared up in Italy, where the younger Simon and Guy had made new lives. Henry of Almaine went to Viterbo in 1271, seeking reconciliation, but the brothers murdered him in church. Both met bad ends, in prison or on the run. A year later, the Lord Edward's accession, while away on Crusade, went off peacefully. His quarter century reign was dominated by his Evesham associates: William de Valence accompanied him to Palestine, and led armies in Wales and Gascony; Mortimer's son continued the family tradition by killing Llewelyn ap Gruffudd, the last native prince of Wales and Simon's old ally; Warenne fought at Stirling Bridge and Falkirk; Gloucester would cause trouble until the 1290s. The great earl himself has made a remarkable comeback. Overlooking his disastrous end as a disgraced foreign adventurer, constitutional historians have celebrated him as a heroic defender of liberty. His name features on memorials at Lewes and Evesham, and graces Leicester University, recalling his intellectual links with Grosseteste.

THE BATTLEFIELDS TODAY

Urban sprawl has affected all the Montfortian battlefields. Modern housing obscures their physical locations, encouraging the historiographical drift to less developed sites outside Lewes and Evesham.

Lewes is most rewarding to visit, with two possible battlefields, the priory, and a castle. Restored in 2009, the latter is open daily, its southern motte and barbican providing spectacular views. The adjacent museum displays a tapestry commissioned for the battle's 750th anniversary. Beyond the railway in Southover, the priory ruins are open to the public. Its grounds also feature a remarkable helmet-shaped monument, celebrating the battle's constitutional significance. Narrow gateways into Lewes and Southover High Streets provide a useful control for the numbers of men who could have defiled through them to fight in the battle.

The revisionist battle site lies along Western Road; see the Ordnance Survey's *Landranger* map sheet 198 or *Explorer* 122 reference TQ4010. The site of Snelling's Mill, just west of St Anne's Church, is marked by a cast iron plaque. From here it is possible to appreciate the proximity of the royalist forming-up area to the barons' position on the hill above the prison. Spital Road forks right from Western Road, past the prison. It is better, however, to approach the downs via The Gallops, an open stretch of grass alongside Spital Road, a remnant of the gentle slope that proved fatal to King Harry's men. A public footpath continues through scrubby woodland veering right past a reservoir towards the traditional battle site at Landport Bottom (map square: TQ3911). This is a designated area of outstanding beauty, a sign board proclaiming it the place where Parliament was won. See the Battle of Lewes website at www.sussexpast.co.uk for directions.

Evesham is less well favoured. A busy road cuts the battlefield in half, and suburban housing obscures the view on either side; see *Landranger* sheet 150 or *Explorer* 205 (map squares: SP0345/SP0445). The area fought over is largely private land, but it is still possible to walk up the

Enzo Piazotta's sculpture in the grounds of Lewes Priory, commissioned for the battle's 1964 anniversary, refurbished for its 750th anniversary. The scene facing the camera is Richard of Cornwall's surrender at Snelling's Mill. (Author's photograph)

The Gallops at Lewes: a remnant of the slope up which the royalists charged. In the middle distance the castle and St Anne's Church show the short distance between the town and the revisionist battle site. (Author's photograph)

main road to appreciate the slope. Thanks to the Simon de Montfort Society, Battle Well is accessible via a marked trail (not a public footpath), and interpreted by a sign board. If Dr Cox is correct, this lies north of the battle's climax, which was nearer the junction of Croft Road and the A4184. The site of Evesham Abbey is a riverside park. The only pre-Reformation remains are the churches of All Saints and St Lawrence, and the bell tower, which post-dates the battle. Two monuments commemorate the events of 1265: a Celtic cross in the south-east corner of St Lawrence's churchyard near Simon's original grave, and an oblong plinth on the site of the abbey's high altar. The Almonry Heritage Centre nearby has a Battle Room dating from 1965.

Rochester and Kenilworth castles are in the care of English Heritage, their keeps providing splendid views. Fragments of Kenilworth's priory and water defences remain east of the castle, along a public footpath. Little remains of medieval Northampton, beyond a relocated sally port in Westgate. St Andrew's Priory is built over, but the river bank is a public park. The Friends of Northampton Castle maintain a website, www.northamptoncastle.com, with a virtual reconstruction of the castle and Victorian images of its demolition.

A Celtic cross erected in 1918 to mark Simon's original resting place near the Abbey wall. The inscription reads: 'Flower of all knighthood … Protector of the people of England'. (Author's photograph)

FURTHER READING

Essential starting points for military students of the Second Barons' War:

Carpenter, D. A., *The Battles of Lewes and Evesham 1264–5* (1987)

Cox, D. C., *The Battle of Evesham – a new account* (1988)

Laborderie, O. de, Maddicott, J. R., Carpenter, D. A., *The Last Hours of Simon de Montfort* (2000) – EHR CXV pp. 378–412 – including a translation of the new source

Treharne, R. F., 'The Battle of Northampton, 5th April 1264', *Northamptonshire Past and Present*, ii (1955), 73–90

The above have largely superseded earlier accounts and their derivatives. Older studies discussed in the text include:

Barrett, C. R. B., *Battles and Battlefields in England* (1896), pp. 37–57

Blaauw, W. H., *The Barons' War, including the Battles of Lewes and Evesham* (2nd edn, 1871) – available online with much original material translated

Burne, A. H., *The Battlefields of England* (1950), pp. 46–53 (Evesham)

——, *More Battlefields of England* (1952), pp. 100–14 (Lewes)

Oman, O., *The Art of War in the Middle Ages* (1924), I, pp. 421–41

Brief histories and plans of major fortifications featured appear in:

Brown, R. A., *Rochester Castle, Kent* (1989)

Godfrey, W. H., *Notes on Lewes Castle and other Ancient Buildings in Lewes with Plans* (1926)

——, *Lewes Castle* (1949)

Morris, R. K., *Kenilworth Castle* (2006)

Biographies of leaders are in the *Dictionary of National Biography* (OUP):

Knowles, C. H., Gilbert de Clare, Earl of Gloucester and Hereford, 11, pp. 746–50

Maddicott, J., Simon de Montfort, Earl of Leicester, 38, pp. 801–9

Prestwich, M., Edward I, 17, pp. 809–24

Ridgeway, H. W., Henry III, 26, pp. 449–72

Smith, L., Roger de Mortimer, Lord of Wigmore, 39, pp. 391–94

Vincent, N., Richard, Earl of Cornwall, 46, pp. 702–12

For the medieval art of war see:

Bradbury, J., *The Medieval Archer* (1996)

Brooks, R., *The Knight Who Saved England: William Marshal and the French Invasion* 1217 (2014)

Keen, M. (ed), *Medieval Warfare: A History* (1999)

Morris, J. E., *The Welsh Wars of Edward I* (1901)

Prestwich, M., *Armies and Warfare in the Middle Ages, the English Experience* (1996)

Hamilton Thompson, Prof. A., *The Art of War to 1400* in *Cambridge Medieval History* IV, Ch. xxiii (CUP, 1929) – obsolete but indicative of traditional attitudes

Verbruggen, J. F., *The Art of Warfare in Western Europe during the Middle Ages* (2002)

Contemporary sources are plentiful but difficult to access. Many were published in the 19th-century Rolls Series (RS) numbered 1–100 as below. Titles are listed as identified in the text, with relevant page numbers. See Carpenter pp. 71–73 for a discussion of their comparative value.

Battle Abbey: printed in C. Bémont, *Simon de Montfort* (1884, Paris), pp. 375–80

Dunstable Annals: ed. H. R. Luard in *Annales Monastici*, vol iii (RS 36, 1866), pp. 229–32, 239

Evesham: Bodleian Library, Oxford manuscript Laud Misc. 529, ff. 70–71

Furness Chronicle: ed. R. Howlett in *Chronicles of the Reigns of Stephen, Henry II and Richard I*, vol ii (RS 82, 1885), pp. 541–44, 546–49

Gervase of Canterbury: *The Historical Works of Gervase of Canterbury*, ed. W. Stubbs (2 vols, RS 73, 1879–80), pp. 234–38, 243

Gilson fragment: J. P. Gilson: 'An unpublished notice of the battle of Lewes', *English Historical Review*, xi (1896), pp. 520–22

Guisborough: *The Chronicle of Walter of Guisborough*, ed. H. Rothwell (Camden Society, 1957), pp. 188–96, 198–202

Langtoft: Chronicle of Pierre Langtoft, ed. T. Wright, vol ii (RS 47, 1868), pp. 136–47

Lewes: Blaauw, W. H. 'On the early history of Lewes Priory...' *Sussex Archaeological Collections*, ii (1849), p.28: translation of Lewes Chronicle

Melsa Chronicle: *ChronicaMonasterii de Melsa*, ed. E. A. Bond, vol ii (RS 43, 1866–68), pp. 138

Oxnead: *Chronica Johannes de Oxenedes*, ed. H. Ellis (RS 13, 1859), pp. 200–3, 206–8

Rishanger: unqualified: *Chronicon de duobus bellis de Lewes et Evesham* published as an Appendix to Walsingham's *Ypodigma Neustriae* attributed to William Rishanger, ed. H. T. Riley (RS 28–27, 1876), pp. 513–28, 535–44

Chronicle: *Chronica Monasterii Sancti Albani Willelmi Rishanger Quondam Monachi*, ed. H. T. Riley, vol i (RS 28–2, 1865), pp. 25–29, 33–37

Trinity: Trinity College, Cambridge manuscript R5/40 f.75

Walsingham, Thomas: *Ypodigma Neustriae Quondam Monacho Monasterii Sancto Albani Conscriptum*, ed. H. T. Riley (RS 28–27, 1876), pp. 152–55, 157–59

Waverley Annals: ed. H. R. Luard in *Annales Monastici*, vol ii (RS 36, 1865), pp. 356–57, 362–65

Westminster: *Flores Historiarum*, ed. H. R. Luard, vol iii (RS 96, 1890), pp. 258–61, 264–65

Wykes, Thomas: *Chronicon Vulgo Dictum Chronicon Thomae Wykes*, ed. H. R. Luard in *Annales Monastici*, vol iv (RS 36, 1869), pp. 143–52, 162–75

Translations of some contemporary narratives appear in:
Rothwell, H. (ed.), *English Historical Documents* 1189–1327 (OUP, 1975)

GLOSSARY

Banneret	Baron or senior knight with his own banner (see conroi)
Chevauchée	Mounted raiding expedition
Conroi	Troop or 'banner' of 10–20 knights/sergeants
Cinque Ports	Confederacy of Channel seaports, originally five in number
Destrier	War horse
Eschiele	Squadron or 'battle' of 100–120 knights/sergeants
Fee	Landed estate held against military service; also fief
Gambeson	Padded protective jacket used by mounted or foot troops
Haubergeon	Short mail shirt, sometimes hooded, used by foot troops
Hauberk	Long mail shirt with hood used by mounted troops
League	Ambiguous measure of distance equal to 1 or 3 miles (1.5–5km)
Marcher	Anglo-Norman magnate or knight resident on Welsh border
Murage	Local taxation used for building town walls
Palfrey	Gentleman's riding horse
Pourpoint	Padded linen jacket, *see* gambeson
Poitevin	Someone from Poitou, south of the Loire
Rouncey	Poor-quality riding horse or pack horse
Seneschal	Steward of great house, hence deputy for absent lord
Sergeant	Mounted or foot soldier of non-noble origin
Templar	Knightly monk, member of the religious order of the Temple

INDEX

Page numbers in **bold** refer to illustrations, maps and their captions.